ROSCOMMON

with Dan Dooner

HERO BOOKS

PUBLISHED BY HERO BOOKS
LUCAN
CO. DUBLIN
IRELAND

Hero Books is an imprint of Umbrella Publishing
First Published 2023

ISBN: 9781910827758

A CIP record for this book is available from the British Library

Cover design and formatting: jessica@viitaladesign.com
Photographs: Sportsfile

★ DEDICATION ★

To all those who have worn the Primrose and Blue

★ CONTENTS ★

★ ACKNOWLEDGEMENTS ★

I HAVE BEEN a keen supporter of the Primrose and Blue ever since completing my permanent transfer from Dublin to Roscommon in 2013. Standing on the terraces in Dr Hyde Park, MacHale Park, Tuam, Salthill and even Croke Park, I have cheered with delight and sighed with heartbreak, like the rest of the Rossies. Blow-in though I am, the county has welcomed me and my family, and I'm proud that my children will grow up here.

I was honoured when Liam Hayes and Hero Books called on me to write this book. I realise that recording the footballing memories of those who have worn the fabled jersey is a serious responsibility, and it's not a project I have taken lightly. I would like to thank Liam for putting his faith in me, and for affording me the opportunity of speaking to some of the finest footballers to have ever played the game. I hope that you, the Roscommon football family, enjoy reading this book as much as I have writing it.

Sadly, I don't believe a book such as this can ever truly be 'complete', not when it is published without the input of some of Roscommon's most famous sons. I can only hope the likes of the late, great Jimmy Murray, Gerry O'Malley and Dermot Earley would approve of it, and perhaps get a kick out of some of the memories shared by those who were no doubt inspired by them.

It would have been an impossible task to speak to every Roscommon footballer deserving of a place in this book, but rest assured, I did my very best to cover as many of the big days as I could, from league games on waterlogged pitches in Tralee to Connacht final pitch invasions in a sun-drenched Hyde Park. Thankfully, there is far more sunshine than storm clouds within these pages!

On that note, I wish to express my heartfelt gratitude to the 25 men who contributed the 'game' of their life. I hope they enjoyed the process as much as I did. It was an honour to listen to their stories but also a privilege to get to know them over the course of the last year. They can add one new fan to the many they have undoubtedly acquired over the course of their illustrious playing careers.

A big thank you also to my former colleagues at the *Roscommon People*. I left with a heavy heart but will always remember the support you gave me throughout my time at the paper and throughout my involvement in this project. A big thank you also to my colleagues at Shannonside Northern Sound.

I want to also acknowledge the support of both my own family and the Ryan family. This book is dedicated to the memory of both my mother, Brigid, and Anna's godmother, Helen O'Keeffe. Helen was a true Rossie, and her gentle presence is sadly missed. My mother was a Dub through and through, but with a definite soft spot for Roscommon. There isn't a day that goes by that I don't miss her.

Last but certainly not least, a very special thank you to my wife and proud Rossie, Anna, and my wonderful son, Noah. I hope that you are as proud of me as I am of both of you. Thank you for your love, support, and above all, your patience over the last 12 months.

Dan Dooner
August 2023

'I have learned that attitude is more than ability; that the motives you have are more important than brains; the courage you have is much more important than all the ingenuity you can gather… and that the most important thing is that your heart is in the right place'

– Dermot Earley

PAT LINDSAY

KERRY 1-6 ★ ROSCOMMON 0-9
NFL Division One Final
Croke Park, Dublin
MAY 12, 1974

★ **KERRY:** P O'Mahony; D O'Sullivan, P O'Donoghue, D Crowley; G Power, P Lynch (0-1), G O'Keeffe; J O'Keeffe, J Long; P Spillane, M O'Sullivan (0-1), J Walsh (0-1); J Egan (1-0), S Fitzgerald, M Sheehy (0-2). **Subs:** F O'Donoghue for Spillane, P Ó Sé (0-1) for Fitzgerald.

★ **ROSCOMMON:** P Whyte; H Keegan, **P Lindsay**, G Mannion; A Regan, D Watson, J Kerrane; M Freyne, J O'Gara; J Kelly, D Earley (0-3), M McNamara (0-1); J Finnegan (0-2), T Heneghan (0-2), T Donlon (0-1). **Subs:** H Griffin for Kelly, P O'Callaghan for McNamara.

##

I WAS ONLY 24 years of age in 1974 and working as a prison officer at Loughan House near Blacklion in County Cavan. That was a great part of the country with plenty of lovely people. I felt blessed to be there. I had broken into the Roscommon senior team four years previously, in 1970. In fact, I made my debut against Kerry in Tralee. Not a bad way to start!

Four years on from that cold and wintry day in November, we had qualified for the National League final against the Kingdom at Croke Park. I think it may have been the first time for Roscommon to reach a National League final, and we were going up against a great Kerry team aiming to win their fourth title in-a-row. Roscommon, on the other hand, have only ever appeared in three finals, winning one against Cork five years later, in 1979.

Both sides had endured disappointing championship campaigns in 1973. We

THE ACTION

★★★★★

REFERRED TO AS 'The Great League Robbery' by some sections of the media, the National League title of 1974 was ripped from Roscommon's grasp by a last-gasp fisted goal from the great John Egan, as Kerry just about lived to fight another day.

Despite their first-half dominance, the Rossies found themselves trailing by 0-4 to 0-2 at the break. Perhaps it was the conditions, or maybe it was nerves that had the Connacht team trailing at the interval, but whatever it was it was soon rectified on the resumption.

Points from Tom Heneghan and the great Dermot Earley brought them level, before they switched on the after-burners to surge ahead. Further scores from Heneghan, Earley (two frees) and Jimmy Finnegan gave Roscommon a richly deserved 0-8 to 0-4 lead by the 47th minute and with the promise of more to come in the remaining 13 minutes or so.

In fact, such was Roscommon's dominance in that second-half, Kerry didn't register their first point until the 53rd minute, a close-range Jackie Walsh free. With just one minute to go, Finnegan had stretched Roscommon's lead to three again following another Kerry point, and the Connacht side finally had the finish line in their sights. That was, of course, until Egan arrived around the square to smash the ball past Padraic Whyte and shatter Roscommon hearts everywhere.

The replay two weeks later saw the great Kerry team regain their composure to ease home on a scoreline of 0-14 to 0-8.

★★★★★

had been knocked out of the Connacht Championship at the semi-final stage by Galway, while Kerry were well beaten in the Munster final by their fierce rivals Cork. There was no 'back door' or 'Super Eights' in those days, of course, so when you were beaten that was you gone for the year. Cork went on to win the All-Ireland final that year... beating Galway in the final!

I suppose it would be fair to say then that both teams had huge points to prove going into that league campaign of 1973-74. But before that, both Roscommon and Kerry had been invited out to America to play in a series of games. Now, don't ask me what that was all about, but it was a very enjoyable trip from a Roscommon point of view. It was the first time the team really got together for any length of time, and it allowed us to bond. It was an excellent team-building exercise, if nothing else.

While we were in the United States, there was also some football matches to be played and we put in a fantastic performance against Kerry in Gaelic Park and managed to beat them. That was a huge result for us. I remember the journey home on the plane. We were all sitting around having a drink and a chat, and discussing what it meant to play for Roscommon. We all knew it was an honour to represent our county, but each of us agreed that simply pulling on the jersey wasn't good enough. 'Let's go and win something,' was the general feeling that night as we flew over the Atlantic. I think it was pretty much decided there and then that we were going to put absolutely everything we had that year into winning the National Football League.

That year's league campaign was very much different to what you see now. The fixtures were split over the back end of one year and into the start of the following one, a bit like the English soccer season. Both Divisions One and Two were split into A and B sections. Roscommon and Kerry were in Division One Group A, alongside Offaly, Cork, Galway, Wicklow, Longford and Tipperary. Very few of those teams are still playing Division One these days!

Both teams lost just once throughout the entire season, but Kerry topped the group because we had also drawn a game. We would play Sligo from Group B in our semi-final while Kerry faced Tyrone. It took us two attempts to get past our neighbours; the first game ended 0-12 each at Croke Park, but we won the replay by four points in Castlebar. Our reward was a league final meeting against Kerry at Croke Park that May. The Kingdom had hammered Tyrone in their semi-final. It promised to be a huge challenge for us, and we were under no illusions that we were going in as rank outsiders. Croke Park in May is a million miles from Gaelic Park in the autumn!

The weather is one thing that sticks in my mind when I think back to May 12, 1974. It was a very wet day, and the conditions were extremely difficult for football. Despite this, we played magnificently throughout. Both teams played good football, in fact. We had some great players in Roscommon at that time, and I mean *great*. That word gets thrown around a lot these days but there's no doubt it applied to men like Mickey Freyne, Dermot Earley and, of course, Tom Heneghan, who would go on to be our manager from 1978 onwards. Tom was playing in the unusual position of full-forward that day, but still managed to chip in with a couple of scores. I can't remember too many better displays from a Roscommon team in all my years involved in and watching football. It was one of the great performances.

It could have been so much more too. We were winning by nine points to six and time was already up. Kerry launched one last desperate attack and the ball arrived high in on top of our defence. The great John Egan, who has since passed on sadly, was waiting for it as it dropped, and he rarely missed! John was a fabulous footballer in a county full of them. He was one of the great forwards. He just threw up a fist instinctively that day and flicked the ball to the net to earn Kerry a replay they didn't really deserve.

The game had ended in a draw, but for us it felt like a heart-breaking defeat. We had dominated from start and almost to the very finish. This was the great Kerry and we had outplayed them at Croke Park. It was a bitter one to take, and leaving the pitch that day it felt like one that got away.

The replay was played a couple of weeks later, on May 26, and our worst fears were realised. We just couldn't replicate the level of performance from the first day out and Kerry ran out comfortable winners in the end to complete a four in-a-ow.

I'll always remember the first match though, because for most, if not all of that game, we were on a huge high. We were not only competing against Kerry, but we were beating them too. John Egan's goal was a real hammer blow at the end of an enjoyable and relatively successful league season.

I thought I played well in that first game but to me the overall team performance was all that really mattered anyway. I was always happy when my team won, and I really didn't give a hoot after that, if I'm honest.

I had marked Seamus Fitzgerald across both games, and I did pretty well against him as far I can remember. You won't hear me saying I was great or anything like that, but I was reasonably satisfied with my performances.

Playing Kerry in any final at Croke Park is never easy and that year was no different. They were a wonderful team with a huge history and footballing tradition, of course. Even the modern-day teams, the likes of Dublin, Galway, Tyrone, Armagh will say it's always a great achievement to beat any Kerry team. I've great admiration for Kerry football too, but it is also very enjoyable when you beat them!

I suppose the one good thing about the core of that 1974 team was that we stayed on together and got to enjoy the years of success which followed from 1977 to '80. I think it was a great compliment to the lads at that time for how they stuck at it and really gave everything for the jersey during their years of service. They did Roscommon proud and provided a lot of great memories for our wonderful supporters.

My Roscommon career would eventually finish in 1985, the same day as the late, great Dermot Earley. We played at Hyde Park against Mayo that day and Dermot was carried shoulder high from the pitch by the Mayo lads at full-time. Again, we had a very good side that year and had beaten a good Galway team down in Tuam.

Both Galway and Mayo had excellent teams in those days and when we won our four Connacht titles in-a-row, we beat one or the other every year, which was a fantastic achievement in itself.

We went into the Connacht final against Mayo that year as very strong favourites, but I think after the Galway game a little bit of apathy or complacency spread through the team and we felt we were going to win handy enough.

Mayo were the up and coming team at that stage and travelled up to the Hyde and beat us very well on the day. They had an excellent team and we just had to hold our hands up. That was the end of the road for both Dermot and myself. Call it a disappointing day or a sombre day, but it was just one of those things. That's the way sport is. You have your good days, your bad days… and that was a day when we were beaten by the better team, and we had no excuses.

While it was a tough way to bow out, and it would have been nice to send Dermot off into retirement with another Connacht medal, the great days live far longer in the memory. The first of our 'four in-a-row' arrived in 1977. I won an All Star that year, but my abiding memory will always be the two days out in Croke Park in our replayed All-Ireland semi-final. They were just fantastic.

In the first game we were winning by six points with just 10 minutes to go. Armagh came back at us and scored two goals in the last few minutes, and we were lucky enough to hang on for a draw in the end, really. They went on to beat us by a single point in the replay – another one of those 'if only' days in Roscommon football.

Again, despite coming out on the wrong side of the result, I thought the replay was a great game. We were playing in front of a huge crowd and there was a great atmosphere, even though there was massive disappointment at the full-time whistle.

Winning an All Star was an honour, of course. The way I see all these individual accolades is that it's very nice to receive an award and I was very grateful for it. But nothing beats winning a Connacht title, a league title, or even an All-Ireland as a team. It's just that extra bit special because everyone's involved.

While we never managed to make it over the line in the 1974 National League final or those exciting All-Ireland semi-final matches against Armagh in 1977, I will always be extremely thankful that I was part of those famous Connacht title-winning Roscommon sides. I was lucky to win an All Star, but I was absolutely blessed to be part of some of this fine county's greatest-ever teams.

MICKEY MENTON

ROSCOMMON 1-12 ★ GALWAY 2-8
Connacht SFC Final
Dr Hyde Park
JULY 10, 1977

★ **ROSCOMMON:** G O'Dowd; H Keegan, P Lindsay, T Heneghan; T Donnellon, R O'Beirne, D Murray; M McDermott, E McManus; D Earley (0-9), M Freyne (1-2), T McManus (0-1); J O'Connor, P Cox, **M Menton. Subs:** M Keegan for Heneghan, J O'Gara for McDermott, M Dolphin for Cox.

★ **GALWAY:** G Mitchell; L O'Neill, J Dillon, M Judge; P O'Neill, B Corbett, J Hughes; TJ Gilmore (0-2), W Joyce; L Sammon, B Talty (2-1), T Naughton; J Tobin, J Duggan, G McManus (0-5). **Subs:** D Smyth for Sammon, K Clancy for Tobin, I Barrett for O'Neill.

"

THE 1977 CAMPAIGN really began the year before when Tony Whyte from Clann na nGael took over as manager. We reached the Connacht final that year, and we drew with Galway, 1-8 apiece in the first ever Connacht final to be played at Dr Hyde Park. The replay was fixed for Tuam, and the weather conditions couldn't have been any more different, let me tell you. The Hyde had been baked in hot sunshine, while Tuam was wet and windy – it was absolutely miserable! It was fairly miserable on the scoreboard too and we were well beaten by 1-14 to 0-9.

But the journey started from there, and we were in good spirits going into Division One of the National League for 1976-77, and while we didn't qualify for the final, we managed to beat Dublin at Hyde Park early on. The Dubs were the reigning All-Ireland champions under Kevin Heffernan after beating Kerry in 1976, so that was a big scalp for us.

THE ACTION

★ ★ ★ ★ ★

THERE'S NO DOUBT that the Connacht final of 1977 was a significant milestone in the fabled history of Roscommon football as it signalled the emergence of the county's greatest team since the back-to-back winning All-Ireland champions of the 1940s.

The final was played at Dr Hyde Park in blistering sunshine. Conditions were hardly ideal for a hard running, end to end battle, but that's exactly what the 20,000 or so people in attendance were treated to. Both sides looked intent on attacking from the off, but it was Galway who held the early upper hand, thanks mainly to two rather soft goals scored by the impressive Brian Talty.

Galway, who had been playing against the wind in that first-half, went in at the break 2-4 to 0-4 to the good, however the Rossies re-emerged like a team possessed and Galway's five-point lead was wiped out after just six minutes. The inspirational Dermot Earley started the comeback, before the tireless Mickey Freyne darted between Galway defenders and slammed the ball into the roof of the net. A minute later, Tony McManus pointed the equaliser, and the Hyde was rocking for the Rossies.

Galway regained the lead through a couple of Gay McManus frees midway through the second-half, but it was clear Earley would not be denied and he led from the front with a clinical display of shooting – and Freyne stepped forward with a point a minute from time to wrestle the Nestor Cup from the Tribesmen.

★ ★ ★ ★ ★

That league campaign and the previous year's Connacht Championship run were the foundations of what we achieved over the next couple of years, really. The championship was straight knockout back then and if you lost, you were out. There was no back door or qualifiers or anything like that. The summer could be over fairly lively if you weren't up to it!

I was working away as a tiler back then, and that's what I'm still at now! I was 24 in 1977 and had been around the panel since around '73, getting the opportunity to play a few league games here and there. I started off playing in the half-back line and then moved up to the half-forward line and, later on, to the full-forward line. They were moving me further away from my own goal the older I got!

I probably preferred playing in the half-back line because that's where I played all my club football for Roscommon Gaels. But it didn't bother me if they stuck me in at corner-forward or anywhere else, I just wanted to be part of the team.

It was great to be involved with those Roscommon teams. We had a great panel back then and we were completely loyal to each other, just a very united bunch. We also really wanted to achieve. Looking back, we should have won five Connacht titles in-a-row. We had a real opportunity to win that 1976 final at the Hyde, but we just let it slip.

Teams trained hard back then... probably not to the levels or with the facilities they train with now, but we always put in a huge effort. We were fully committed too, and even though we enjoyed a couple of pints, nights out drinking or anything like that were very few and far between.

We began our championship run that year with a three-point victory over Mayo in MacHale Park. Beating Mayo in Castlebar was always an impressive result and I scored a point in our 0-16 to 0-13 win. We probably weren't as impressive in the semi-final, but we were comfortable enough winners over Sligo. 'Jigger' O'Connor and Eamonn McManus scored important goals to set up another Connacht final against Galway.

There was a 'home and away' agreement between Galway and ourselves, so the 1977 final was played at Dr Hyde Park because the '76 replay, the last championship meeting between the two counties, had been played in Tuam.

There must have been around 20,000 people at the Hyde that day, and they were treated to a thrilling match in fine weather. We didn't get off to a great start and we conceded two very soft goals in the first-half. Both were quite similar too. Galway had a fast start when Brian Talty blocked Harry Keegan's clearance down and put the ball in the net. His second goal came from another block, this time on Richard O'Beirne... and the ball just seem to dribble into the net past our goalkeeper Gerry O'Dowd.

We had our own chances too and Mickey Freyne, our inspirational captain that day, missed a penalty in between the two Talty goals. So, things weren't looking too good for us at half-time, five points down.

It was a completely different game in the second-half. We left the dressing-room determined not to lose another Connacht final, particularly in front of our own supporters. We realised we only had the second-half to get a result and there was a fierce Roscommon response to a disappointing first-half.

Galway's five-point lead disappeared very early on as Dermot Earley and Tony McManus scored good points, and Mickey Freyne made up for his penalty miss with a goal. We were playing much better by then. The memory of losing in 1976 was always on our minds and we just felt we had to win that day to make up for it.

But Galway never give up, and it looked as though we were heading for another replay in Galway, before Mickey Freyne stepped up again to score a lovely point. He was brilliant that day and put in a real captain's performance. The final whistle went shortly after that, and there was just a great feeling of relief. It was definitely a monkey off our backs to win a Connacht title. We had been waiting a long time since 1972, and before that we hadn't won one since '62. Little did we know what lay in store for us over the next four years!

As for my own performance that day, I was marking Johnny Hughes from Mountbellew. Johnny would go on to play a good few more years after that final. It might be a different story in modern football with the amount of statistics and the video work teams do, but back then I was only concentrated on the team performance and making sure I did my job well. I don't have many memories of specific moments in games, just that for each time the ball came into your sector, you had to make sure to win your duel. That wasn't easy on a hot day in July 1.

Johnny was a strong player too, and it was obvious why he was picked for the Galway team for a number of years after that. We were quite similar players in certain ways when it came to our positions on the field. It's interesting that in the 1976 final Johnny played at wing-forward and I was at wing-back, and by the time the '77 game came around we had both switched.

Like my teammates, I was only interested in winning the match and there was plenty of concern when we got off to that slow start. I always felt confident because we had a good team. Tony McManus was only starting out and he had been on the bench for the 1976 final. He got on the scoresheet that day at the Hyde with a lovely point. It was a very impressive scoresheet that day too… Dermot Early (0-9), Mickey Freyne (2-1) and Tony McManus (0-1). Most counties would love to have three players of that quality chipping in for them.

We were the better team that day, in my opinion, so I knew we would find a way back into it. The final score was 1-12 to 2-8 in the end, but I felt we should have won it by more. We left a lot of shots short; our shooting accuracy wasn't as good as it should have been. There's no doubt we could have made things easier for ourselves!

The tradition back then was to go to The Royal Hotel in Roscommon town for a meal after matches. You'd also have a couple of drinks too, but I don't remember any real big drinking sessions around then because we had an All-Ireland semi-final to play not too long after that. We were drawn against the winners of Ulster that year in the semi-final, so we all went and watched the Ulster final a couple of weekends later.

Armagh came through it with ease, beating Derry 3-10 to 1-5. Noel Marley, All Star Paddy Moriarty and Larry Kearins scored goals that day for them. I read somewhere years later that Derry officials had travelled in the opposite direction a couple of weeks before for our final. They were going for three Ulster titles in-a-row, and they must have been very confident. Armagh were rank outsiders, but they had a really good team.

When it came to our meeting in the semi-final, it was another case of what might have been for Roscommon football. We played two very exciting games at Croke Park. The first match ended in a draw – 3-9 to 2-12 – and we lost the replay two weeks later by a single point. We should have won that semi-final. We were the width of a post away in both games, really. I hit the foot of the post in the first game, and then struck the crossbar in the second. So close.

I think if we had beaten Armagh that year and reached the final against Dublin then we would have won that All-Ireland final in 1980. I just think we would have had that experience of the big day out at Croke Park under our belts. The 1979 semi-final was another missed opportunity, and if either one of those campaigns ended with a final in Croke Park it would have helped us in '80 against Kerry.

But that's how it goes sometimes...

I continued playing right up to that final in 1980. Time was moving on by then and I think that team was breaking up anyway. I was also getting married around that time, and so it was time to step back.

I look back very fondly on my time with Roscommon and consider myself extremely fortunate that I got to play in one of the county's most successful periods. I also togged out with the likes of Dermot Earley, of course, and Mickey Freyne, another Roscommon great. We had Tony Mac and John O'Gara too, who I believe was one of the best midfielders the county ever had. He was certainly the best midfielder I played with in my time anyway.

I probably wouldn't have considered myself up to their standard... I just worked hard on my football and deep down was just delighted to be part of it. The years have passed now, and I have great memories to look back on, playing football all over the country with some great friends.

You couldn't ask for anymore. To top it off with an All-Ireland would have been nice, but sure look, that's just the way it worked out for us.

SEAMUS HAYDEN
(& DES NEWTON)

ROSCOMMON 1-9 ★ KERRY 1-8
All-Ireland U-21 FC Final
Dr Hyde Park
OCTOBER 15, 1978

★ **ROSCOMMON:** B Kenny; **D Newton**, P Dolan, S Tighe; G Connellan, R O'Beirne, E Egan; **S Hayden**, G Fitzmaurice (1-0); M Finneran (0-1), G Emmett (0-4), C Reynolds; A McHugh, H Crowley (0-2), T McManus (0-2). **Sub:** A Dooley for McHugh.

★ **KERRY:** C Nelligan; M Keane, V O'Connor, M Spillane (0-3); G Lynch, J Mulvihill, G Casey; J O'Shea (1-0), S Walsh (0-1); T Bridgeman (0-3), D Higgins (0-1), J McElligott; P Foley, E Liston, P Sheehan. **Sub:** D Coffey for Sheehan.

66

I CONSIDERED MYSELF lucky to play at under-21 level for three years. There were quite a few of us in that boat too. We were there or thereabouts when it came to winning titles in 1976, '77 and then '78. The difference in the latter two years was Tom Heneghan. He was an established county senior footballer at the time, and he took over the under-21 team.

In 1977, we had lost the Connacht final to Leitrim. That was certainly something we hadn't expected but Leitrim were a very good team at that time. The result was a bit of a shock to the system, but in fairness, they went on and came very close to beating Kerry in the All-Ireland semi-final. They had a lot of very good players so perhaps it shouldn't have been a shock!

As is always the way at underage level, we lost a number of very good players after that 1977 final, including the likes of John 'Jigger' O'Connor, Gay Sheeran,

THE ACTION

★★★★★

IT REMAINS, 45 YEARS on, one of the greatest days in the proud history of Roscommon football. A day when Roscommon overcame a star-studded Kerry side to win an All-Ireland title. A day when Tom Heneghan's young warriors toppled the Kingdom.

Roscommon's under-21s put the disappointment of losing the Connacht final to Leitrim in 1977 behind them. They embarked on a thrilling championship campaign in '78, culminating with this dramatic victory over a Kerry side who were chasing a four in-a-row of All-Ireland titles.

This victory was made all the more remarkable considering the Kerry side featured five of the team that had captured yet another senior championship just a few weeks before against Dublin. Names like Charlie Nelligan, Vincent O'Connor, Mick Spillane, Ger Lynch, Jack O'Shea, Seanie Walsh and Eoin 'Bomber' Liston would strike fear into the hearts of most teams.

There were brilliant Roscommon performances all over the field, and they perhaps should have been further ahead than 0-6 to 0-2 at half-time. Seamus Hayden and Gerry Fitzmaurice were proving more than a match for their illustrious opponents at midfield, and it was Fitzmaurice who scored Roscommon's only goal in the second-half.

Roscommon were left hanging on a bit by the end thanks in part to a Jack O'Shea goal for Kerry, but spurred on by their loyal supporters, they managed to see off a late Kingdom onslaught to win only a second All-Ireland under-21 title and a first since 1966.

★★★★★

Danny Murray and some of the other lads who were now overage.

Thankfully, Tom Heneghan stayed on as manager for the following year. I think he got a bit of a land in 1977 when he saw how well Leitrim did in the All-Ireland series and realised that we weren't too far away from the required level. He instilled a great sense of belief in us, and we trained very hard ahead of the new season. It's hard to overstate Tom's importance to us because he was instrumental in the success we had that year.

Of course, we were a bunch of 19 and 20-year-olds and we probably didn't give too much thought to the fact that Tom had been playing for Roscommon for seven or eight years. The man had been around the block, and he knew what it would take to get us to the next level.

That defeat in 1977 made us realise we'd need to put even more effort into training and matches, and so we were happy when Tom decided to resume training earlier than normal the following year. That hard work must have made the difference because we ended up winning a lot of our games in 1978 by very narrow margins. We won the Connacht final by a point against Galway (3-9 to 2-11) and the All-Ireland semi-final by a point against Down (0-8 to 0-7 at Dr Hyde Park), and then we ended up winning the final by a point against Kerry also. They were fine margins that could have gone the other way too. Winning those types of games requires real energy, commitment, a will to win, and also a fear of losing, I would say.

It really helped that the whole county got behind us that year too. Inside the camp, we knew we had a good bunch of players because we had won the Connacht minor final in 1975. We were well beaten by Kerry in the All-Ireland semi-final then, but the nucleus of this team came from that. There were quite a number of players who then played at under-21 level in 1976 and '77 before our final year at underage in '78. The quality was certainly there because a lot of that team would also go on to play senior football, where they won Connacht titles and weren't too far off winning an All-Ireland at that level.

The set-up had come an awful long way in the two years since 1976, that's for sure! Myself, Tony McManus, Micheal Finneran, and a few others were playing at that stage and the whole thing was a bit of a joke. There was just no organisation to it at all. I remember we were beaten by Galway at the Hyde that year. There was no preparation; we were all just gathered together to tog out and play. Little wonder we were beaten!

That all changed under Tom. He brought huge levels of organisation and preparation to the panel. The days of cobbling together 15 lads for a championship match were long gone by the time 1978 rolled around. It was some transformation in just two years.

I definitely remember the excitement building with each game that year. There was very little chat about us after our first game or two, but when we reached the Connacht final word started to get around. *Hold on, this is a talented group.*

It also helped that the final, against Galway in Ballinasloe, was a very good game of football. Suddenly, the crowds attending our matches started to grow, and we relished playing in front of them too. Thinking back, it was ideal preparation for the move to senior football the following year.

Football was the talk of the county in the late 70s... and I suppose it still is! The senior team started to enjoy sustained success, winning back-to-back Connacht titles in 1977 and '78. They had also played in All-Ireland semi-finals in those years so had a taste of Croke Park and playing against teams like Armagh and Kerry.

Our under-21 team was back in the middle of an All-Ireland campaign just a few weeks after the senior side lost to Kerry in their semi-final at Croke Park. Those were exciting times to be part of Roscommon teams and there were some great days out for our supporters. The mood around the county was very positive and those same supporters were tuned into this young team because they knew something exciting was happening.

As positive and as happy as everyone was, we still had to face a formidable Kerry team just a couple of weeks after their seniors had put five goals past Dublin to win another All-Ireland final! The Kerry under-21s weren't too bad either and they were going for four All-Ireland titles in-a-row themselves. They were very hot favourites to beat us.

There was quite a big gap between our semi-final against Down and the final with Kerry. We had beaten the Ulster champions by 0-8 to 0-7 at the Hyde all the way back in September. The delay was caused by the involvement of five Kerry under-21 players with the senior team. Their semi-final against Louth was only played in October, just two weeks before the final was scheduled to take place.

Kerry beat Louth by two points in Drogheda, so they clearly weren't too fazed by the loss of any home advantage. That probably came back to haunt them in the final!

How we managed to get home advantage for that All-Ireland final was another story, or maybe a few other stories! I believe a lot of the credit for that must go to Micheál O'Callaghan, who was our chairman at the time. This was 45 years ago and there were different strokes being pulled back then!

To make things more complicated, both counties had also qualified for the Ceannaras final, which was a competition played between the four senior provincial champions at that time. There was talk of a coin toss to determine the venue for both matches, but there were also rumours that Kerry would compensate Roscommon for the delay in the under-21 final being played…

Let's just say that Micheál was a good negotiator, and he was well respected within GAA circles. I think he talked to the GAA hierarchy and to the chairman of the Kerry County Board at the time.

Maybe it went something like this… 'Look lads, ye're on a high. You're after winning the All-Ireland and you're going for your fourth under-21 title in-a-row. You're playing our young lads in the final so wouldn't it nice to have the two finals at Hyde Park?'

Whatever Micheál said to them, it was some coup for Roscommon football and it made for a great occasion in the county town in the middle of October. Home advantage or not, it was always going to be a daunting task for any Roscommon team.

Some of those Kerry lads were already household names… Eoin 'Bomber' Liston had just scored three goals and two points against the mighty Dubs at Croke Park! There was serious talent everywhere you looked… Charlie Nelligan in goal… Vincent O'Connor captain… Jack O'Shea and Seanie Walsh at midfield… a real formidable outfit. The only question people were asking in the build-up was, *How in the name of God will Roscommon cope with these guys?*

We were under no illusions as to what we were up against, and it wasn't difficult to keep our feet on the ground because no one really gave us much of a chance anyway! But we had Tom Heneghan in our corner, and he was to have a perfect day – both on the pitch and on the sideline – on October 15, 1978!

The Ceannaras final was the curtain-raiser for the under-21 final and Tom lined out at corner-back that day against the likes of Mikey Sheehy, Pat Spillane, John Egan and 'Ogie' Moran. The atmosphere was electric at the Hyde. I can still hear it now… *We are Ros! We are Ros! We are Ros!* Real hairs on the back of your neck stuff.

The seniors won their match by eight points or something like that, and the crowd just got louder and louder after that. The Hyde was a cauldron that day and the poor Kerry supporters were outnumbered by about 10 to one! We used all this as major motivation, of course. I remember talking to Peter Dolan, our full-back, and a clubmate of my own with St Joseph's. He had the 'honour' of picking up Bomber Liston for the day and I never saw a man as motivated to put in a performance.

To this day, I still believe it was whole-hearted endeavour and just so badly wanting to prove ourselves that won that title for us. Maybe with such a strong team and players already winning senior All-Ireland medals, Kerry felt all they had to do was turn up on the day? I don't think they knew what had hit them later that evening. They had come togged for a game of football while we were geared up for war!

At that time there wasn't really the same media focus on senior All-Ireland finals never mind the under-21s. There weren't any mobile phones either, of course, so there was far less talk about big matches. I remember just training very hard in the build-up to it and that we were all in great shape. I was looking forward to the challenge of playing against those Kerry lads again. I had played against Seanie Walsh and Jack O'Shea at minor level, and I knew what we were up against.

It was myself and Gerry Fitzmaurice at midfield, and I remember we were in the dressing-room beforehand when Tom Heneghan arrived in. The sweat was still dripping off him after starting in the Ceannaras final which was still going on outside.

'Right lads, let's go and win this All-Ireland…'

He was a great motivator and the few words he said to us in the dressing-room were just what we needed before going out onto the field. I said a few words to lads after that too.

I spoke to Peter Dolan again just before we went out.

'Today is your day.'

I was on Jack O'Shea, and Fitzmaurice was marking Walsh. We had one final chat just before the ball was thrown in. 'This is our chance,' I said to him, 'We might not be as well-known as these boys but let's make sure they know what they're up against'.

We were lucky in that we had forwards like Gerry Emmett, Micheal Finneran and Tony McManus, so I knew if we got enough ball into them that they'd do the rest. It was a team effort though and we had a very strong full-back line and a good, solid goalie in Brendan Kelly. We also had a strong and mobile half-back line, while Fitzmaurice and myself wouldn't be wanting for a lot in the middle of the field. Up front, we had forwards who had been training with the seniors. We certainly weren't as naïve as some people around the county might have thought.

I vividly remember the feeling of sheer relief at the full-time whistle. We had been going pretty well and Fitzmaurice had scored a goal to give us a five-point lead at one stage. It was a low-scoring game but that suited us. The momentum started to shift a bit in the second-half though and my man, Jack O'Shea, got through for a goal. That hurt me deeply at the time. I thought, *That won't happen again.*

The relief when the referee blew that whistle, and we were a point ahead was extraordinary. Then our supporters flooded onto the pitch, and we were mobbed in all the excitement.

I remember going over to collect the cup off the back of a lorry trailer and saying a few words. The presentation though was totally irrelevant to me, really. What mattered was that we had achieved what we had set out to do. We got over the line and that's what it was all about. It was no trouble to us to celebrate, of course, but winning the game was what mattered.

It was peak satisfaction winning an All-Ireland title with a group of lads that had put so much effort into it over a number of years. It's a day I and the other lads on that talented team will never forget.

★ ★ ★ ★ ★

DES NEWTON

66

MOST PLAYERS WILL tell you they find it difficult to remember specific moments from a match, and even my memory of the under-21 All-Ireland final would be fairly limited. Also, there are no video clips of that match available anywhere because there was no television coverage of it back then. That's unthinkable nowadays!

To try and jog your memory, you nearly have to go back through old newspaper clippings, rooting out previews and reports of the match from the local papers. The *Herald* and the *Champion* gave that final a great amount of coverage. But some of my best memories are of the build-up to the match itself.

I was actually only a minor that year and so I wasn't at any of the Connacht Championship matches! We were beaten by Mayo by two points at the Hyde in the Minor Championship in July, and they went on to beat Dublin in the All-Ireland final. I was marking a guy called Tom Byrne in that Connacht minor final and he actually came on against Dublin and scored two vital goals.

After losing to Mayo, I thought my county football was finished for the year, in only the first week of July. I was four years younger than many of those under-21 players and I didn't really know any of them, let alone play in any of their matches. But as far as I can remember, they were operating with a very small panel that year. I think they only had something like 21 players available to them throughout that Connacht campaign. That's nearly the size of most senior backroom teams these days!

After they won the final, Tom Heneghan and his selectors obviously decided it would be safer to pull in a few players in order to make up the numbers in training. I happened to be one of those players. There were lads pulled in even later than I was, guys like Liam Tierney from Elphin, Paul Collins from Shannon Gaels, my own club at the time, Gerry Watson from St Dominic's. They were only a year out of minors at that stage.

I was only turning 18 at that time but I knew a few of the fellas from neighbouring clubs, like Gerry Connellan from Kilmore, and Coman Reynolds from Elphin. There were also lads like Gerry Fitzmaurice, Seamus Hayden and Tony McManus, who were part of the senior setup… I would have been standing back in awe just being in the same dressing-room at some of those guys.

We trained at the Hyde, but the spectator stand hadn't yet been built in 1978. There was a grass bank on the Athlone Road side of the ground and one of the training drills Tom Heneghan used to make fellas do was carry other guys on their back up that bank. I remember carrying Gerry Fitzmaurice up that bank. Gerry was a grown man at that stage, and I was still only a cub really!

I also remember doing 400-metre runs at the end of those training sessions. I would have had to drop out because I hadn't trained seriously for 10 or 12 weeks after the Minor Championship. Tom Heneghan kept me back after training finished and made me do 10 laps of the pitch! There was no favouritism or special treatment just because you were young. If you were part of the set-up you were expected to perform at the same level as everyone else.

We played Down in the All-Ireland semi-final at the Hyde. I was a substitute, and it was a terribly wet day. If you look back over those match programmes, subs were very rarely used back then. I think there was only one substitution made in that semi-final and I'm not sure if there were many made in the final against Kerry. If you didn't get picked for the starting 15 you had very little chance of getting on the pitch barring a serious injury. You could only use three subs and the culture at that time was that once you were on, you stayed there for the full match. There was no such thing as tactical changes or bringing 'impact subs' off the bench in the last 20 minutes.

The semi-final was played on September 10, and I would have only been on the panel for around two weeks by the time it came around. There was no expectation of getting on the field or anything like that, I was just happy to be involved.

Kerry had reached the senior final that year and beat Dublin easily. Eoin 'Bomber' Liston scored three goals in that game. Because they got to the senior final, I think there was an agreement between Kerry, Roscommon and the GAA that the under-21 final would be postponed for a couple of weeks. Maybe in order to compensate us for that, Kerry agreed to come to Roscommon to play the final. Whatever the reason, I presume the fellas who didn't have a lot of medals on that Kerry team would later regret the game being played in Roscommon town.

Maybe the lads with senior medals from September didn't mind either way!

Both senior teams were playing in the Ceannaras final that day too and I suppose that was also part of the decision process when it came to where the game would be played. Traditionally, that match would have been played at an earlier date but I think it was also delayed due to the All-Ireland final, and so they decided to stage both on the same day.

We were training three nights a week and at weekends as well. The seniors had also been doing a bit of training for the Ceannaras and I used to hitch to and from Sligo, where I was attending college. I used to get a lift to the home house from Gay Sheeran, stay the night, and then my father would leave me on the road to hitch back to Sligo the following morning. It was fairly full on! I did that for about three weeks even though I had no expectation of playing in that final.

We played a challenge match in the Hyde against the seniors the week before the final. The team was then picked the following Tuesday evening, and, lo and behold, I was named in the starting 15 with Mickey Murray dropping out. Mickey was the legendary Jimmy Murray's son from Knockcroghery. I guess it showed how ruthless Heneghan could be because Mickey had played every minute of every game up to that point. He had won Player of the Year with the minors the year before, so I'm sure missing out on that final was very hard for him.

The other thing I remember in the lead up to the game is that Peter Dolan had a shoulder injury. The newspapers the week before carried a lot of speculation about what would happen if Peter couldn't play. The general feeling was that I might go to full-back and Michael Murray would play at corner-back.

There was an infamous article in the *Irish Independent* the Tuesday or Wednesday before the game, which basically said that if Roscommon were going to play me at full-back they hadn't a hope in hell. *They might as well go to Lourdes and play the game!* They questioned why Roscommon were going to have a completely inexperienced minor marking Eoin Liston, who had just scored three goals in the All-Ireland senior final. I was sitting in Sligo library reading the paper when it came out. Peter Dolan was fit enough to play in the end but if I needed any more motivation, I got it that morning reading the *Indo*!

I was busy the week of the final. I had an interview for a teacher training college in Cork and so I wasn't in Sligo that week. I got my place on the course thankfully, but everything was all kind of coming together for me at the wrong time really.

As for the game itself, the papers said there were around 10,000 or 12,000 at it. That would have been a very big crowd at an under-21 match at that time. It would have been a big crowd for the Hyde back then anyway because there had been no development of the county ground at all. You had two sidelines and grass banks, basically. It was definitely the biggest crowd I had played in front of up to that point. It was quite intimidating coming out on to the pitch for the warm-up. Even getting our picture taken… I couldn't remember playing on a team where I got my picture taken before a game. Looking at the picture now, we were a fairly bedraggled looking group… I don't think those shots were done as professionally as they are nowadays… or at least that's what we'll tell ourselves, anyway!

I was very aware of the crowd, and the atmosphere and all that prior to throw in. I was marking Padraig Sheehan. I think of the seven senior players who started that game for Kerry, at least five of them had played from the start against Dublin in the All-Ireland final and one came on as a sub. You were looking out the field at lads like Jack O'Shea, Sean Walsh, Tom Bridgeman, Charlie Nelligan, Ger Lynch, Tom Spillane. Fellas you were watching on television a few weeks beforehand were now standing a few metres away from you on the pitch!

The seniors winning the Ceannaras Cup before us that day was very important. They all walked through our dressing-room on the way to where they were getting togged out. You had the Lindsays, Keegans, Dermot Earleys, that calibre of Roscommon footballer walking through and wishing you well. It might not have been a big deal to the likes of Tony McManus who was by then training with them most nights, but to me it was huge. To have my hand shaken by Dermot Earley… my childhood hero… before I went out and played an ALL-IRELAND FINAL! That was massive and it remains one of my treasured memories from that day.

Even without the added motivation from a national newspaper article, I was always determined to make a big impact on the game. Football back then was very much a man-on-man contest, and your primary job was to make sure your man didn't score. Things were obviously going my way in the first-half because I remember Sheehan hitting me! He was probably getting a bit sick of me standing so close to him. I was a bit winded and went down on one knee. The crowd were going mad over in the corner because they had seen the incident. Unfortunately for Sheehan, one of the umpires saw it too and the referee was called in to book him. My father used to always say to my brother, John and I that if a fella reacts like that then you know you have him. He would have received similar treatment during his playing career, so he knew what he was talking about! That incident gave me a lot of confidence, because then I knew I was doing my job well.

Peter Dolan, who was an injury doubt before the game, did get hurt in the second-half and I remember him walking in around behind the goal to get to the other side of the pitch for treatment. I stepped in to mark Liston for a couple of minutes. I remember that very well and I also remember being very glad when Peter came back onto the pitch again! My man was taken off around that time – he was the only change Kerry made in the game. That showed me I had done my job really well because players being taken off just didn't happen back then.

The weather wasn't great that afternoon and the pitch was already heavy from the senior match beforehand, but I felt we were in control most of the way through. Kerry did throw everything at us in that second-half, but we managed to repel them. Every little bit of pressure we put on them, like forcing them to kick a wide or just making sure you got as near to them as possible, edged us on to the final whistle. They got a bit of a fortunate goal near the end and that could have been very deflating for us but not even that could derail us. We had plenty of leaders in the team and we were urging each other on to see out the game. Kerry had come back from around five or six points down at one stage and eventually got to within a single score of us. But we battled on right until the full-time whistle.

When that final whistle went, I just remember falling onto my knees. The first person out onto the pitch to me was Donal Keenan from the county board, a man who had been President of the GAA just a couple of years previous. He picked me up off the ground and it was just pure mania after that really. There was a truck pulled up in front of the old dressing-rooms and the presentation of the cup took place on the back of that. We were all up on that truck… I'm sure those Kerry players and their county board officials who agreed to playing it at the Hyde didn't quite know what to make of it all!

As a back, it's difficult to remember your individual performances. Forwards score goals and points and it probably makes it easier for them to remember games. But

I do remember there was a very nervy finish to the end of that match. I remember Donal running on and also my dad catching up with me afterwards which was hugely important to me. I certainly don't remember much about the celebrations that night, but it wasn't because I was drinking. I had just turned 18 a few weeks before and I didn't take a drink for years after that either. It was, however, one of the few times my dad had a couple of drinks!

We met up in Castlerea the evening after the game and we did a whole tour of the county in just one night. It was absolutely mad! I may not have been drinking but there were a few pit-stops along the way for the more senior fellas! It was great going to your own club. We went to Croghan and to Glancy's Bar where there was a patch of open ground at the time. There was a truck set up for us there too. It was an awfully long night! My celebrations were cut short because I had to travel to Cork for college on the Wednesday morning. I wasn't home again for a month after that, and all the excitement had died down a bit by then... just about!

I was one of those players who won that All-Ireland while still a minor and so I thought it was going to happen every year. But I played three more years after that at under-21 and didn't even get to a Connacht final, never mind anything else! We were beaten by Mayo the following year, and by Galway in 1980.

The final against Galway was a tough game personally because I was badly injured in it. I had been a sub for the Connacht senior final the weekend before and then got injured in the under-21 game and missed out on the rest of the All-Ireland Senior Championship. I didn't get to experience Croke Park on All-Ireland final day and didn't get that runners-up medal. So that Galway game proved to be a very costly match for me.

All-Ireland finals come around very rarely in Roscommon, and you have to take your chance when it's presented. And I guess another player had to be very disappointed for me to have my starting place on the team. I often look back on that. Michael Murray and I know each other well. It must have been very hard on his father too... to have your son play all the way through and then not to feature in the final. I don't think they ever held it against me though. It just showed Heneghan's ruthless streak. That was something I encountered at the first training session I went to when he made me run those laps around the pitch. It didn't matter that I was only 18, I was still carrying fellas like Gerry Fitzmaurice on my back!

99

GERRY FITZMAURICE

ROSCOMMON 0-15 ★ CORK 1-3
National Football League Final
Croke Park, Dublin
MAY 13, 1979

★ **ROSCOMMON:** J McDermott; S Tighe, P Lindsay, T Heneghan; **G Fitzmaurice**, T Donnellan, D Murray (0-1); D Earley (0-7), S Hayden; T McManus (0-2), J O'Gara (0-1), S Kilbride (0-1); M Finneran (0-1), M Freyne (0-2), E McManus. **Sub:** Richie O'Beirne for Heneghan.

★ **CORK:** B Morgan; S O'Sullivan, K Kehilly, B Murphy; J Crowley, C Ryan, J Kerrigan; J Courtney, V Coakley; D McCarthy, J Barry Murphy (1-0), D Allen (0-2); P Cavanagh, D Barron, C Kearney (0-1). **Subs:** T O'Reilly for Coakley, M Mullins for McCarthy, J Coleman for Crowley.

66

I WAS NEW to the Roscommon senior team in 1979. We had just won the All-Ireland under-21 championship the year before, and I had thought that that was me done with football, to be quite honest. Then one day I got a call from Tom Heneghan to go and train with the senior panel. At first, I thought I'd just be going in as a substitute or as part of the extended panel.

We had a game coming up against Derry, and I was at home and got a call to join up with the team because someone was injured. I was just on the panel for the Sunday, but I was very happy. I was just chuffed with myself to be even called up for Roscommon. I arrived up there, walked into the dressing-room, and suddenly I'm handed a jersey and told I was going to be playing at half-back. It was a bit of a shock, but I didn't really have enough time to think about it, which was probably a good thing at the time!

THE ACTION

★★★★★

IN 1979, ROSCOMMON were regarded as one of the best football teams in the country having won two Connacht senior titles in-a-row, as well as an All-Ireland at under-21 level the year previous. A national title at senior level was the next challenge and Tom Heneghan's charges duly delivered with one the finest performances in the history of Roscommon football.

The first point of the final, which was played in front of 31,000 people in Croke Park, went the way of Dinny Allen and Cork, but the tide turned shortly after and, amazingly, the Rebels didn't trouble the scoreboard for another 24 minutes. Points from the likes of the colossal Dermot Earley, Tony McManus, Mickey Freyne, and Sean Kilbride helped Roscommon into a 0-8 to 0-2 lead at half-time.

The Rossies were rampant that afternoon and by the 17th minute of the second-half the game was effectively over as a contest as they surged into a 0-13 to 0-2 lead. Cork did manage a goal through the legendary Jimmy Barry Murphy, but it wasn't enough to halt the Primrose and Blue tide. Dinny Allen missed a penalty late on as Roscommon saw out a comfortable win in the end.

The Roscommon supporters made up the majority of the crowd that day and they swarmed onto the hallowed turf as Pat Lindsay lifted the county's first national title in 35 years.

★★★★★

We won that game as far as I can remember. I was marking Gerry McElhinney, who was also a Northern Ireland international soccer player and, even more worryingly, an accomplished boxer too!

From that match, we went straight into the league campaign and, suddenly, I was playing against Kerry in a quarter-final in Croke Park, a team I never thought I'd play against… at a venue I never thought I'd play in! It was definitely a daunting experience, but I was playing on an excellent team full of great players, so that helped of course.

At that time, I was togging out next to some of the great names of Roscommon football; I couldn't believe my luck. Harry Keegan, Pat Lindsay, Tom Heneghan, Dermot Earley, Danny Murray who I had played under-21 with, Tom Donnellan, and up front you had the likes of Tony McManus. I was a bit overawed by the whole thing, a bit starstruck. Could you blame me, really?

Kerry were the best team around at the time but we beat them at the quarter-finals stage. We also defeated Offaly, another very good outfit in the semi-final. We just managed to get the better of the two of them by a point or two. They were two very tough games but also a great way of learning on the job for a young player at the beginning of his senior career.

The final was against Cork, and there were a lot of wonderful footballers involved in that game. The Rebels had a fine team back then too; in fact, there didn't seem to be too many weak teams knocking around in the late 70s. It was a great era for Gaelic football. Every game was a tough battle and the conditions for league games were rarely conducive to good football anyway!

Winning a National League Division One title for Roscommon would be a huge achievement even today, but you tried not to think about it too much in the build-up to that game in 1979. I was fully concentrated on my job on the day of the final itself. I was marking Dinny Allen and that was the only thought in my mind at that time.

I remember starting the match with the fear that Dinny would get away from me in those opening minutes and kick a couple of scores. He scored the first point, and that's the last thing you want as a back on an occasion like that. Dinny was quite quick, and he had the accuracy to go with it as well.

I was lucky I was surrounded by top-class defenders. I knew I didn't have to worry about controlling the match or doing anything too fancy; I could just concentrate on my own position and stopping Dinny from having too much influence on proceedings.

I must have done relatively okay, because Dinny was moved away from me later on in the match. Not that my new man was any easier to deal with! But again, I knew I had the players around me. Tom Heneghan was marking Jimmy Barry Murphy, and then you had Pat Lindsay and Harry Keegan close by too. God, I'm glad I wasn't a forward operating in that area! Those men were so in control.

They were confident in their own abilities and physically very strong. It was no wonder we dominated a talented full-forward line that day. It's strange, but I remember more about my teammates' performances that day than I do about my own. It was probably because I spent most of the game standing back and admiring them!

I can only imagine what the county would be like nowadays if Roscommon qualified for a national final, but back then there wasn't as much exposure in terms of the media and that. There were rarely any replays or highlights of league matches either... so you could have a really bad game, and everyone would have forgotten about it by the time the next one came around!

We played the game, and it might be on the telly, or then again it might not. There was no controversy over *GAAGo* or anything like that back then! Most of the people who wanted to watch the match would have had a ticket and gone along to see it anyway.

The local newspapers were the biggest part of the coverage. You had the *Roscommon Champion* and the *Roscommon Herald* around at that time, so it was whatever they decided to do in the run-up to the match that got people talking. It was difficult enough though if you were a nervous fella going into a game like that without having cameras and microphones shoved into your face!

In Roscommon, there was already a great feeling about the team at that time among the players, officials and the supporters. It all felt like one big family, and so there was huge excitement whenever the team played. The Hyde was always full for our home games, with people coming back to the county for the weekend from work or college or whatever in Dublin and Galway and other far-flung places.

Whenever we were playing in Dublin… well EVERYONE came out for it. The streets around Croke Park turned Primrose and Blue, and the supporters were up for the whole weekend, not just for the game itself!

That final in Croke Park will live long in the memory of many of the Roscommon supporters around at that time and, of course, the players who were involved on the panel too.

We went out to put on a performance that day, and man, that team was majestic! Every single one of the lads played wonderfully and it was just a joy to share such a hallowed pitch with them. Winning the league title was an incredible feeling, especially because it came just months after I had joined the senior ranks, and just a year on from winning the All-Ireland under-21 title. I thought this was the norm for a Roscommon footballer! Of course, there was mad excitement around the county, and wherever Roscommon supporters gathered too. There was great joy and celebrations that night in the Spa Hotel in Lucan where the team and some, or perhaps most of our supporters, were staying.

That was a *wild* night! There were hundreds and hundreds of Roscommon people trying to get into the hotel and the staff were taken completely by surprise. Supporters were sneaking in through rooms and toilet windows to try and get down to the banquet, where we were all in full flow.

The following day was great too as we arrived back in Roscommon for a victory parade in the town. Budgets were tight back then, of course. You'd get the togs and socks, but you had to return the jersey after each match and there were no training tops or hoodies or anything like that. I think we got a pair of boots the following year for the All-Ireland final, and we might have got to keep the jersey too… if only we had won it! There was no Club Rossie bus or anything like that back then either, so we were all put in the back of an open trailer and up and down the town we went, waving at everyone we saw! All in all, it was a great couple of weeks for the county and for our people.

My dad had sadly passed away a few years prior to that 1979 final. My family was quite young at the time, so I ended up back at home helping my mother to run the family business. We had a bar and grocery store, so that was my life back then. Other than that, I played football, with a bit of rugby thrown in during the winter too.

I never, ever believed I'd get to play senior football for Roscommon. You had Dermot Earley on that team, sure… the man was an icon! That was the standard back then. I felt I was lucky to get on the under-21 team the year before, but never dared believe I was good enough for the seniors… and to be honest, I still don't! But when I was called up, I really appreciated it, and by God I enjoyed every minute of it.

If that call from Tom Heneghan never came, I still would have played club football and been happy to do so. I had that under-21 medal and felt that wasn't too bad for a fella who never thought he'd kick a ball for a Roscommon team.

I was truly honoured to play for the county, and I don't say that lightly. It opened up a whole new life to me. I came from a small town on the border, but representing Roscommon brought a lot of new friends into my life. Suddenly, I had a huge panel of friends. One thing about Roscommon is that you keep up those friendships and I've remained close with those lads for the past 30 or 40 years.

We still have meetings, and get together every couple of years. The county is small, so we'd see each other at matches and play the odd game of golf together too. There's a great camaraderie still with all those players.

I suppose the family-run bar we own is a help with that too. We're right on the road to Castlebar, so when it's championship time during the summer we'd have people dropping by for a pint or two on the way home. You're always meeting people and I'm grateful that it has led to so many great friendships.

I feel very lucky to have won both an All-Ireland medal and a National League medal. I came in at a great time; there were fellas about 20 times better footballers than I ever was, but were playing in teams that just didn't allow them to showcase what they could do. I landed in a team that had just won two Connacht senior titles and I then got to win two provincial titles too, and even play in an All-Ireland final. It was a glorious era for Roscommon football, and I managed to just fall into it.

I was lucky and I've never forgotten that.

99

TONY McMANUS

ROSCOMMON 2-20 ★ ARMAGH 3-11
All-Ireland SFC Semi-Final
Croke Park
AUGUST 10, 1980

★ **ROSCOMMON:** G Sheeran; H Keegan, P Lindsay, G Connellan; D Murray (0-1), T Donnellan, G Fitzmaurice; D Earley (0-3), S Hayden; J O'Connor (0-4), J O'Gara (0-1), A Dooley (0-1); M Finneran (1-8), **T McManus (1-2)**, E McManus. **Subs:** M McDermott for Hayden, M Dolphin for E McManus.

★ **ARMAGH:** B McAlinden; D Stevenston, J McKerr, K Rafferty; B Canavan (0-2), J McCorry, J Donnelly; J Kernan (0-2), C McKinstry; P Moriarty, J Smyth (1-0), F McMahon; M Murphy (1-2), B Hughes (0-1), P Loughran (1-4). **Subs:** S Devlin for McKinstry, N Marley for McMahon, H Kernan for Loughran.

66

THE BUILD-UP to that semi-final in 1980 was really super. I was studying at college in Dublin in those days and that was all part of the fun really, with the travelling up and down to training twice and three times a week. It was tough and there were sacrifices to be made, but those were magical days.

I suppose to put it into some context, that period from around 1977 to '80 was one of the great eras of Roscommon football, and supporters and former players like me still speak about it to this day. We won four Connacht titles and were knocking on the door in the All-Ireland Championship too. We also won an All-Ireland under-21 title against Kerry in 1978, so it was a very successful period for us at all levels.

Armagh had already beaten us in an All-Ireland semi-final in 1977. The first game that year had ended in a draw before the Orchard County eventually beat

THE ACTION

★★★★★

ROSCOMMON HAD JUST won their fourth Connacht title in-a-row, putting up some big scores in the process, including a 3-13 to 0-8 demolition of Mayo in the final. They had also won the National League just the year before.

The Orchard's midfield duo of Joe Kernan and Colm McKinstry were on top early on and corner-forward Martin Murphy laid down the gauntlet for the Connacht champions with a goal after just 12 minutes. The Rossies warmed to the challenge as the first-half went on, however, and with Micheal Finneran, John O'Connor and Tony McManus to the fore, were well in contention as half-time approached.

Disaster struck however just five minutes before the break when a harmless looking Jimmy Smyth shot slipped through goalkeeper Gay Sheeran's hands to give Armagh a commanding 2-6 to 0-7 lead.

Roscommon manager, Tom Heneghan, had kept his players back at half-time, as referee Seamus Aldridge frantically blew his whistle to call them back out onto the pitch. When the Rossies did return, it was certainly worth the wait as they put on an awesome exhibition of attacking football, scoring 2-13.

Micheal Finneran hit an incredible 1-8, while Tony McManus was also in fine form hitting 1-2, including a superb goal to level matters midway through the second-half. With the comeback complete, Seamus Aldridge's full-time whistle sparked scenes of jubilation in the stands where Roscommon supporters could finally celebrate their first All-Ireland final appearance since 1962.

★★★★★

us by a point in the replay. I suppose that made what happened three years later all the sweeter. We also suffered semi-final defeats to the two kingpins of that time, Kerry in 1978 and Dublin in '79. We were well beaten by Kerry, but the Dubs only beat us by a single point.

Despite those near misses, there remained an aura around that Roscommon team of the late 70s. I had come through the ranks with that group of players and had, and still have, a great affinity with each of them. It was just a golden time to be a Roscommon footballer and we were the four in-a-row Connacht champions by the time we met Armagh again in 1980.

I still maintain the biggest loss that team suffered was the year before against Dublin in that one-point defeat in the 1979 semi-final. To my mind, we wouldn't have lost the 1980 final to Kerry had we managed to get over the line against the Dubs the year before. Now I'm not saying we would have beaten Kerry in the final in '79, but I think the experience of an All-Ireland final would have helped us the following year. I still have no doubt whatsoever that that Kerry team was there for the taking in 1980, but we left it behind us against Dublin the year before and missed out on that valuable Croke Park final experience.

The other thing I remember quite vividly about that time is how our wonderful supporters seemed to grow with that team. Dermot Earley was already an iconic figure in Roscommon and further afield by 1980. He had such charisma and a real presence. The likes of Pat Lindsay, Harry Keegan, our captain Danny Murray… God, I could name them all… but those older guys were the heart and soul of that team. I suppose they were edging closer and closer to the end of their football careers at that point, so an All-Ireland final appearance and a Celtic Cross would have been the icing on the cake for them. They were genuine warriors and fantastic guys to be around and to play football with.

Looking back at that semi-final against Armagh, I would say I definitely had better games myself, but as a team we had really gelled that year and it was absolutely crucial we got over the line in that game and qualified for our first final together. By half-time, our place in that year's All-Ireland showcase was in serious jeopardy, however. There's no doubt we were in big trouble. We hadn't played well and all of sudden, right before the interval, we found ourselves five points down. Things were looking bad for us once more in a semi-final at Croke Park.

You'd always get a bit of banter or even a bit of 'sledging' from your marker, especially if you were a forward! It was never anything too serious and if you think about it, it was actually a compliment that they expended energy trying to put you off your game. It meant they were worried about you.

Though, to be honest, you wouldn't really think of it that way when a big hardy Armagh man was snarling at you. I just tried to keep my head down and concentrate on my football. Whenever I scored, I just made sure to give it back two-fold!

I was marking Jim McKerr that day and there's no doubt he was very much on top in the first-half. And he wasn't shy about rubbing it in either! I remember his welcoming comment to me was something about being a 'Free State so and so'… I knew I'd be in for a tough afternoon!

Jim, to be fair, was a good defender and he kept me scoreless in that half. But the second-half was a different story entirely and I managed to grab a goal and two points to come out on top. Micheal Finneran put me through for my goal, and then I returned the favour to him later on. Between us, we finished with 2-10 of Roscommon's 2-20 total that day, though Micheal had the lion's share with 1-8.

It was a good job the thousands of Roscommon supporters found their voice in that second-half because that was huge in driving us over the line. How could we face them if they went home disappointed after an All-Ireland semi-final again?

Winning that game is something that will always live with me. Scoring a goal in front of Hill 16 in an All-Ireland semi-final is difficult to put into words, really. So is walking off the Croke Park pitch knowing you will be back there playing in an All-Ireland final. I wish I could have bottled that feeling. It was one of the very special days.

I still believe the heartbreak of the previous three years helped drive us on against Armagh that day in 1980. I think the feeling amongst the players and management was that we had no choice but to win… we couldn't miss out on a place in the final again. We also knew we had a lot more to offer and that we just hadn't done ourselves justice in 1977, '78 and '79. That being said, we were extremely lethargic in the opening 35 minutes, as if we were expecting things to just happen for us. Armagh took full advantage of our slow start. When you're sitting in that dressing-room trailing by five points and staring your fourth straight semi-final defeat in the face… well, that does tend to focus minds!

It wasn't like there were changes in personnel or anything like that either; it was more just a change in attitude, really. We knew going back out that we'd have a slight wind behind us in that second-half and that might just help us get to grips in midfield where Armagh were dominating.

We managed to get a bit of momentum early on in the second-half and that was crucial if we had any hope of reeling them in. The injustice of the Dublin defeat was certainly in my head when we re-emerged after half-time, and I think it really drove us all on as we chased down that Armagh lead.

I remember it being a lovely, sunny day and there was an incredible atmosphere in Croke Park. Armagh brought a huge following with them and were probably a bit more vocal, particularly in that first-half. It was a huge occasion, and it can overwhelm you, if you let it.

Luckily, we found it within ourselves to come out after half-time that day and put in a storming second-half and score 2-13. It was one of the great second-half performances. It was still in the balance with just a few minutes left but we finally managed to pull away from what was an excellent Armagh team.

I still get people coming up to me to chat about that game, and that entire era. Obviously, the most difficult conversation always centres around what happened next. Our defeat in that year's final was incredibly hard to take and I would say it still remains a regret for most of us who were involved that year. Yes, 1980 is always the year that stands out in my mind... but not for the right reason in the end!

It is a regret of mine that we never had the opportunity to climb the steps of the Hogan Stand as All-Ireland winners. It leaves a bit of an open wound, or an itch that was never scratched... I don't know what you'd call it! But I've great pride in what I achieved in my football career too, and most of all, I really enjoyed playing the game. Maybe I went on a year or two too long in the end, but I enjoyed the camaraderie and also being competitive. Being competitive was very important to me.

Watching football matches nowadays, I have sympathy for modern forwards because most of them are just crowded out of the game now. In my time, it was very much man-on-man and there were far more 50-50s to contest. I loved that. Now players these days might think the pace of the game was awful slow in the 70s and 80s, but to me it was a more attractive style of football compared to the cautious hand-passing style of today.

It was also more honest and exciting. It was 'me against you', or Jim McKerr or whoever… and no matter what happened or what was said during the match, we shook hands at the end no matter who won.

On that day at least, it was us who came out on top against Armagh.

,,

DANNY MURRAY

KERRY 1-9 ★ ROSCOMMON 1-6
All-Ireland Final
September 21, 1980
CROKE PARK, DUBLIN

★ **KERRY:** C Nelligan; J Deenihan, J O'Keeffe, P Lynch; P Ó Sé, T Kennelly, G O'Keeffe; J O'Shea (0-1), S Walsh; G Power (0-1), D Moran, P Spillane (0-1); M Sheehy (1-6), T Doyle, J Egan. **Subs:** G O'Driscoll for Power.

★ **ROSCOMMON:** G Sheeran; H Keegan, P Lindsay, G Connellan; G Fitzmaurice, T Donnellan, **D Murray**; D Earley (0-1), S Hayden (0-1); J O'Connor (1-2), J O'Gara (0-1), A Dooley; M Finneran (0-1), T McManus, E McManus. **Subs:** M Dolphin for Dooley, M McDermott for Hayden.

WE WENT INTO the All-Ireland final of 1980 having won four Connacht titles in-a-row, but we were under no illusions, and knew we were up against one of the best teams ever in that Kerry side. It was Roscommon's first All-Ireland final since 1962 and we had been beaten in four semi-finals during that time. We lost to Kerry in 1972, Armagh in '77 after a replay, in '78 we were beaten by Kerry again, and then in '79 Dublin beat us by a point. We had plenty of experience, but it mattered that we had never played an All-Ireland final at Croke Park prior to that day in 1980.

I think it's fair to say that ourselves and Kerry were the two best teams in the country at that stage. While we never got over the line in an All-Ireland final, we had won the National League in 1979, beating Kerry in the quarter-finals that year. We then beat a very good Offaly team in the semi-final, before defeating Cork by 0-15 to 1-3 in the final.

THE ACTION

★★★★★

KERRY WERE GOING for a three in-a-row, having hammered Dublin in the two previous finals. They were once again favourites for Gaelic football's showpiece at headquarters.

In the end it was a scrappy affair, with referee Seamus Murray awarding a staggering 64 frees, 41 of those to Kerry. However, when John 'Jigger' O'Connor palmed to the net after just 35 seconds, it looked as though Roscommon were ready to relieve Kerry of their 'kingpins' status. But the reigning champions slowly warmed to the task, and a Mikey Sheehy goal helped them gain parity by half-time.

The second-half started in much the same way as the first, with Roscommon threatening the Kerry goal. Charlie Nelligan had to be at his best to turn another 'Jigger' effort over the bar. The Rossies gave as good as they got right up until the closing stages and could consider themselves unfortunate not to score a second goal through Aidan Dooley. Páidí Ó Sé pulled off an extraordinary block to deny the Roscommon man.

The teams were level by the 57th minute and that's as close as Roscommon have come to an All-Ireland senior title since 1944. There were more missed opportunities in the closing stages and many of those who were there that day still wonder what might have been.

Kerry, however, were unlikely to be denied their 'triple crown' and points from Jack O'Shea and two from Mikey Sheehy helped them over the line against a gallant Roscommon team.

★★★★★

Back in those days, the team selected the captain and so I was elected to the role. It was a huge honour for me. To lead your county out for any match is a privilege, but to lead them out at Croke Park in an All-Ireland final is the pinnacle of any footballer's career. I was only 24 years of age, and there I was leading the Roscommon pre-match parade in front of 65,000 people! That was a great moment for the players and our supporters, and one that will last forever with me, even though we didn't win.

I don't think the final was a brilliant game but our semi-final against Armagh should probably go down as one of the great semi-finals. It was a really high-scoring game and that was a very good Armagh team. It was also a very tough and physical game, and one that would certainly go down as a bit of revenge for our semi-final defeat in '77. Following our win over Armagh, the hype as we built up to the All-Ireland final was something else. It was nearly 20 years since we last reached an All-Ireland senior decider, when Gerry O'Malley was captain against Kerry in 1962. There was a great buzz in the county in the weeks that followed.

I was always one for keeping the head down and just trying to concentrate on the game itself. I preferred travelling alone to games to avoid the media and things like that. As captain, I probably wouldn't be the fella inside the dressing-room banging tables or remonstrating with fellas. We had great leaders throughout the team. Some, like Dermot Earley, Pat Lindsay, Harry Keegan, Seamus Hayden for example, didn't need to be named captain in order to lead their teammates. There were plenty of fellas capable of doing the talking in the dressing-room. I was more of a captain on the field, and I did my best to lead in what I did and how I played rather than shouting at lads or giving rousing speeches.

I must say, we were lucky that we had such an accommodating county board at the time. Micheál O'Callaghan was the chairman, Paddy Francis Dwyer was treasurer, and Phil Gannon was secretary. Then we had Tom Heneghan as team manager, Danny Burke, Gene Beirne, PJ Shine and Liam Martin as selectors, and Ossie Bennett was masseur. The kitman was also important in terms of team spirt and that was Mick Mullen. His son, Donal was mascot on the day too. All of them, the board and team management, worked together to help get the very best out of us. I don't think there can be too many complaints about what we achieved together in those years.

To prepare for the All-Ireland final against Kerry, most, if not all of us, took a week off from work in order to train and get ourselves ready for it. It was very professional, even by today's high standards. We trained at the Hyde in the morning time, then we had lunch, followed by video work in the afternoon. We also had different guests and team managers in to speak to us. I suppose you'd call it motivational speaking nowadays! Everything was geared towards preparing us physically and mentally for the challenge of Kerry.

I was working as an analyst with Bord na Móna at the time and, I have to say, they were very good to me over the years I was with them. Any time I needed time off for football it was never a problem. In 1977 and '80, I was given a total of three weeks off with pay. It was a great position to be in and, of course, it made sure you worked even harder in order to repay that support.

There's been a long association between Bord na Móna and Roscommon football. I later became a manager there for a few years before I retired and we used to take on the Murtaghs, Ciaráin and Brian, for the summer months. In fact, we'd take on 50 or 60 youngsters for the summer. It was great for them and meant they could stay around Ballyleague Lanesboro instead of taking off for somewhere else.

I think the Roscommon and Kerry teams were quite similar in terms of their ability and as a result, the final was a tight and cagey affair. Our tactics were quite simple... take Tim Kennelly away from his central position, and find Tony McManus in the space that was created. In the first 10 minutes or so, we were 1-2 to no score, and the goal had been created by McManus for John 'Jigger' O'Connor. Kerry eventually got wise to this, and Kennelly simply stopped following John O'Gara out the field.

In a tight game like that there are usually a lot of frees given away. We were under strict instructions, however, not to give their talented forward line any space at all. You were walking a fine line for the entire match because obviously they had one of the best free-takers in the country too in Mike Sheehy. It meant your tackling had to be inch perfect, because you couldn't cough up a free anywhere within the 40-yard mark. Sheehy would punish you every time. As it was, he ended up scoring 1-6 of Kerry's 1-9 total that day. So much for best laid plans!

Still though, keeping Kerry to 1-9 was a difficult task. You just had to do your best to get as close to them as possible and annoy them enough without giving up soft frees. We also posed them a similar problem at the other end of the field. Roscommon had some fine forwards like 'Jigger', Micheal Finneran, Tony McManus, and John O'Gara, who had a fine game that day too.

The way the game panned out, probably due to the nerves of All-Ireland final day, meant that there was a lot of kicking into open space. This led to a lot of 50-50 balls and so it was very much man against man. Whichever team won the most of those battles across the field was going to win the match, and that turned out to be Kerry. I still feel that there were a few decisions in that match where we didn't really get a rub of the green at times. I think Michael O'Hehir remarked on it in his commentary too. He didn't see one or two of them as fouls anyway, and I think there were a couple of fair shoulders given as Kerry frees. I don't think referees went out to intentionally favour the dominant teams but maybe there are times when they do get a bit more protection. But I also know I got some of those decisions going my way when I was playing!

I would say it was probably just the way the way the game turned out on the day. It was a very physical game, and we just came out on the wrong side of a few decisions. I know some of the local journalists commented on it in their reports after. But for me, I've always said how important it is to respect match officials. It's a very difficult match to referee, an All-Ireland final. Everyone is very fired up and there's the ultimate fear of losing as well.

In terms of my own performance that day, I was reasonably happy I suppose. Though I did drop one ball around the square, and Pat Spillane latched onto it and fisted it over the bar. I was so disappointed with that. Overall, I wouldn't say it was Roscommon's best performance that year. A lot of people commented afterwards that perhaps we were too robust in our approach. There were also those who questioned why we had changed tactics from the first 10 minutes.

But I think it's only when you're on the pitch do you get a real sense of how a game is developing and that day Kerry had adapted to our early tactics. We also missed a few chances that we would normally put away, particularly in the second-half. But look, some days it goes for you and some days it doesn't.

I was extremely disappointed to lose that All-Ireland final, not so much for myself but for the wonderful Roscommon supporters over those four very successful years. Bringing Sam Maguire home would have been the icing on the cake for them. I don't think any of us will ever forget them; they were absolutely brilliant. The followed us all over the country and the county still has many terrific supporters to this day.

Going into the final, I would have been confident, but I wouldn't say I was overconfident or anything like that. Running out at Croke Park in 1977, I had no fear because we were into the unknown. I got Man of the Match in the semi-final that year. 1980 was different as captain because you know what can happen and that fear of losing does come into the equation. But you don't dwell on it; you're fully immersed in the game and you're thinking about nothing else until that final whistle.

There's always analysis after the game and sometimes it's done too quickly after the full-time whistle. But to think about things like, *I should have done this, or I could have stopped that*…well, you're only really wrecking your own head. I played around 10 years for Roscommon, and I can tell you every game was different. My biggest 'critics' were my own family in terms of feedback! But no matter what you're at, if you don't receive feedback then how else are you supposed to improve?

Sometimes it's negative, while other times it's more constructive. But every player who goes out onto the field knows how well or poorly he played. If he's honest with himself, he knows where he can or should improve and can also take feedback from the people he respects. That's the key… learning how to take that constructive feedback. You'll always get negativity, but I think you're better off putting that out of your mind.

To this day, people still come up to me and say, 'It must have been awful to lose that game?' Of course, it was, but the enjoyment I got from playing during those four years from 1977 to '80 far outweighed that one disappointing day at Croke Park. I was part of a journey with an exceptional group of players. Each and every one of them put in Trojan work during that period. The team management and our county board deserve great credit too. It was the adventure of a lifetime, and I loved every minute of it… right up to that final whistle in 1980.

Looking back, I think we did our county proud. Every one of us did our very best and I think we left everything out on the field that day. I don't think any more could have been asked of that team.

It's now been 43 years and counting since Roscommon's last appearance in an All-Ireland senior final. I believe the current team has great potential to end that long wait. The game has changed since 1980 and the tactics nowadays are very different to the way we played. I think 2023 showed that Roscommon can compete with the bigger counties. They showed they could frustrate a great Dublin team, they're well managed, and a every bit a Division One team. I certainly wouldn't write them off reaching an All-Ireland semi-final in the next couple of years. Hopefully, it won't be too much longer until we see those wonderful supporters turning Croke Park Primrose and Blue once more.

GAY SHEERAN

KERRY 1-6 ★ ROSCOMMON 0-9
National Football League Division One
November 2, 1980
AUSTIN STACK PARK, TRALEE

★ **KERRY:** C Nelligan; J Deenihan, J O'Keeffe, P Lynch; P Ó Sé, T Kennelly, G O'Keeffe; J O'Shea (0-1), S Walsh; D Moran, T Doyle, P Spillane (0-2); B Walsh, E Lison (0-1), M Sheehy (1-2). **Subs:** V O'Connor for B Walsh.

★ **ROSCOMMON:** **G Sheeran**; H Keegan, P Lindsay, G Connellan (0-1); G Fitzmaurice, T Donnellan, D Murray; S Hayden, J O'Gara; E McManus (0-2), T McManus, J O'Connor; A Dooley (0-1), D Earley (0-1), M Finneran (0-3). **Subs:** J McManus for Fitzmaurice, M Dolphin for Hayden, L Tiernan (0-1) for Keegan.

"

THE NATIONAL LEAGUE back in 1980 was organised into four games before Christmas and four games afterwards. Everyone looked forward to the league at the time because it killed the monotony between the All-Ireland final and Christmas. As well as that, if you hadn't been in form in the championship, you had a chance of winning two or three games to stay in the division and set yourself up for after the Christmas break.

We were all in good shape after the All-Ireland final against Kerry in September. We wouldn't have been doing a huge amount of training, just turning up twice a week for sessions.

As soon as the league fixtures were released, the Kerry game in round two was being touted as a big game for us. It certainly was in terms of psychology, because everyone wanted to see how we'd bounce back from the devastating All-

THE ACTION

★★★★★

THE NOVEMBER LEAGUE meeting between Kerry and Roscommon at Austin Stack Park in Tralee is perhaps one meeting between the pair which should never have gone ahead.

Roscommon had stopped overnight in Portlaoise on their way down to the Kingdom, and were forced to disembark at Mallow due to the flooded track. The subsequent bus journey to Tralee, a distance of around 70 kilometres, took two and a half hours due to local flooding.

The match went ahead just 19 minutes later than scheduled despite all the delays and traffic problems, and it was a game Roscommon should have won comfortably. The visitors raced into a 0-5 to 0-1 lead, thanks to the efforts of brothers Tony and Eamon McManus, and Aidan Dooley and John O'Connor.

The Kingdom were a point down at half-time. Pat Spillane fired over twice to give Kerry the lead before the impressive Jack O'Shea extended their lead with a point two minutes later. Roscommon fought back with two points of their own before Sheehy restored Kerry's lead. The visitors had goalkeeper Gay Sheeran to thank for keeping their opponents in sight. He saved what looked a certain point from Pat Spillane with three minutes left.

With time almost up, Roscommon launched one final assault on the muddied Kerry goalmouth in a bid to rescue the situation. Dermot Earley chipped a ball in and eventually O'Connor laid it back for debutant Liam Tiernan, who fired over the equalising point.

★★★★★

Ireland defeat less than two months before. There's no doubt that we trained a little harder in the build-up to our long trip to Tralee!

Ordinarily, when you travelled to somewhere as far away as Kerry for a game, you'd go down the night before. But we had the most unusual organisation for that fixture. We went to Portlaoise on the Saturday and stayed there for the night before continuing to Tralee on the Sunday. It was a funny sort of an arrangement.

At that time, any communication you got for a game was via a card or a letter from the secretary Phil Gannon. Something like... *You are expected to travel with the Roscommon senior team on Saturday for the match against Kerry on Sunday... Meeting in Portlaoise at 3 pm on Saturday.* That was usually organised during the midweek training session.

So, off we went to Portlaoise on the Saturday. I can't remember where we stayed but probably at Declan O'Loughlin's place. I'll never forget the rain that fell that night, it was almost Biblical. But we got the train the following morning, which was a bit of a novelty at the time because it was only the second time we had travelled that way as a team. The first time being to Croke Park for the All-Ireland final.

You'd usually spend the journey chatting and reading the Sunday papers or playing cards. Everyone had their own way of killing time. The younger fellas were more likely to play cards while the older lads would be chatting about the game. Then you'd have the officials who would be busy organising how everything would go when we got down there. Everything was going smoothly until we came to Mallow...

It turned out that the tracks were flooded up ahead and so we'd have to cut the card games short and charter a bus the rest of the way. We had planned to arrive in Tralee at around 12 o'clock because the game would have been as early as two o'clock due to the clocks going back. The flooded tracks would cause a delay.

Everyone assumed the game would be called off at this stage because it was a real winter's day and the rain had been torrential. Not even our officials had a clue what was going on, because back then there were no mobile phones and there was no way of calling ahead unless you were at the train station. The scene that met us upon our arrival wasn't too promising either... we got in at around 20 to two and the fire brigade were there with pumps on the pitch!

I think it was decided the game would go ahead because we'd travelled all that way from Roscommon. It would have been a hell of a long way to go just to be told the game had been postponed. There was no sign of Kerry giving us a walkover either! From what I remember, the fire brigade worked on the pitch right up until 2.15. We weren't allowed out, so we just did our warm-up in the dressing-room.

Thankfully, the rain had stopped by the time we finally got out there. Talk about contrasting scenes between this mid-winter league match and the last time we met Kerry! The pitch was like a sticky bog, and neither side would have been at peak fitness levels at that time of year, so it was a real struggle.

Johnny Maloney from Tipperary, one of the great referees at the time, was in charge that day. He was a sensible man and before the game he was going around telling fellas that he'd pull them up on things that might be dangerous.

Just make sure lads are safe, was the gist of his instructions. Both teams would have been fairly anxious to win that game. Kerry had pretty much the same team from the All-Ireland final, plus Eoin 'Bomber' Liston. Not a bad addition to have really!

We were standing on this water-logged pitch in Tralee and looking out the field at lads like Charlie Nelligan, their full-strength full and half-back lines, Jack O'Shea and Seanie Walsh at midfield, 'Ogie' Moran, Tommy Doyle and Pat Spillane in the half-forward line, and Barry Walsh, Eoin Liston, and Mikey Sheehy in the full-forward line. Our lads might have enjoyed a few games of cards on the train, but Kerry were playing with the full deck!

Kerry don't like to be beaten at home and they would have also wanted to prove that the All-Ireland final was no fluke, so from that point of view, there was a lot on the line. There was less pressure on us than there was in the All-Ireland final, because we were playing away from home in front of a smaller crowd. We felt we were in with a good chance because we believed we could have won the game in September had we played up to our usual standards.

The pitch in Tralee was a problem, however, as we knew it would be the moment we arrived. It was almost impossible to play quick football on it. The game was a very tight affair; the marking was tight, and the hits were *hard*. The football was scrappy enough and there were fellas slipping and sliding all over the place. It required a huge amount of effort to do anything really.

Despite the conditions and our underdogs status, we were well on top until Mikey Sheehy got a goal. I don't remember too much about it; it might have come off Gerry Fitzmaurice. But it didn't matter, because Sheehy was always lethal in those situations anyway. He was the best man to time a run and when he got the ball there was usually nobody between him and the goalkeeper. At that time, you could score with a hand-pass and so as a goalkeeper when you had a forward coming at you, it was difficult to predict whether they would kick it or punch it. Suddenly you're in No Man's Land and… BANG!

The game was tight and at the time there was no 'spare man' or sweeper system. It was man for man all over the field and you just had to win your own ball. Seamus Hayden and Dermot Earley against Jack O'Shea and Seanie Walsh at midfield was a huge battle. I would have been kicking long… while Charlie Nelligan never did anything other than kick it long! At the time, you had two or three lads climbing for it, and the best man won it and moved it quickly into the forward line.

There were huge duels in there too…

Kerry had Bomber Liston inside and we had Pat Lindsay on him. Lindsay wouldn't give an inch, no matter who it was. In fact, he would have looked forward to playing against Liston because he would have primed himself for that match-up in the All-Ireland final before the Bomber was ruled out.

It was a mighty battle. Playing behind them, I got to watch the two of them in action, trying to get out in front of each other. Lindsay was trying to break ball, while Bomber wanted to win it and flash it off to Ogie Moran, Spillane, Sheehy or whoever was running through. Everyone else had to be on their toes too. Gerry Connellan was no slouch either. He was an All Star that year but like everyone else, he was fighting his corner fiercely.

We found ourselves a point down with just a couple of minutes left in the game. It was a low-scoring game due to the conditions and the fact that both teams cancelled each other out, really. 1-6 to 0-8 after almost 70 minutes of football tells you how difficult it was. Not surprisingly, the pitch had got worse and worse as the game went on. In fairness to the referee, within seven or eight minutes of the game starting he had come to me with some sound advice for kick outs.

'Just place it wherever it's dry,' he said. At the time, the ball was restarted from the small square following a wide. But Johnny, being the sensible man he was, told me to place the ball anywhere I could find dry ground.

'Well Johnny, there isn't a whole lot of that around here today,' I said to him. It was such a dreary day. If the place had lights, they would have been on from about 11 o'clock in the morning it was so dark.

By the end, we were just hanging on and hoping to get something out of it. That was looking unlikely when Pat Spillane got the ball between the left half-forward position and the 14-yard line. Spillane glided along the top of the ground, and he was soloing towards our goal. One of our backs got to him, and he just weaved by him, but right towards Pat Lindsay. Lindsay hit him with a shoulder and threw him off balance. Spillane, who was nearly out over the end line, punched the ball goalward and it was heading over my crossbar.

Instinctively, I pushed the net up, knocking the ball back across the crossbar and out into the small square on the far side of my goal. It reached Danny Murray, who carried it up the field before we won the free which eventually resulted in Liam Tiernan sending the ball over the bar. Now, I don't think he ever scored a point for Roscommon before or after that day, but Liam kicked it high into the Tralee sky and it landed on top of the net just over Charlie Nelligan's crossbar.

Meanwhile, at the other end of the field, Pat Spillane was ranting and raving at the umpires.

'Go away you… and don't be annoying us,' I told him. Liam Tiernan's score had levelled the game and meant we would be making the long journey back to Roscommon with an unexpected point. Liam's kick gave the whole team a great bonus for the rest of that league campaign. We went on and beat Offaly, and then after Christmas we won a couple more before losing the league final to Galway.

We were young at that time, some of us… the likes of Tony and Eamonn McManus and Micheal Finneran. Only 23 or 24. To us, it was a big deal get a draw in Kerry, there was no doubt about that. For Dermot Earley, Harry Keegan, Pat Lindsay, Tom Heneghan, and all of those lads who had soldiered for 10 years or more, taking a point off Kerry below in Tralee was something they had never done before. As a team effort, it was one of the biggest performances I was ever part of. They were All-Ireland champions, had just beaten us two months before, and had their full team out on their own pitch.

It was a massive result.

There was no real time for back-slapping, however, because we had to get the bus back to Mallow! We then got the train to Portlaoise, picked up our cars and headed home. It was great to be with the group on the train back before we went our separate ways in Portlaoise. The only thing you could listen to at that time was RTÉ Radio and the sports results weren't as easy to get as they are now.

But I remember feeling great when I got home. We could face the rest of the week knowing that we had gone down to Kerry and got *something*.

Even Dermot Earley was emotional after that game. He, Harry and Pat and all those lads who had played with Roscommon for years, had faced Kerry so many times without ever really getting the better of them. To them, that result must have felt like a win. It's for that reason I look back on that game as the 'Game of my Life' because it was such a great team performance against all the odds.

A result against Kerry in Tralee, playing alongside some of the greatest footballers ever to wear the Primrose and Blue. It's hard to beat that!

99

HARRY KEEGAN

ROSCOMMON 1-5 ★ GALWAY 1-8
Connacht SFC Final
Dr Hyde Park
JULY 13, 1986

★ **GALWAY:** P Comer; J Fallon, G Dolan, S McHugh; E Guerin, T Tierney (0-1), A O'Shea; B Talty (0-1), V Daly; R Fahy (0-1), G McManus (0-1), P Kelly (0-2); B Brennan, B O'Donnell (0-1), M Brennan (0-1). **Subs:** M Coleman for Guerin, R Flaherty for Fahy, S Joyce (1-0) for McManus

★ **ROSCOMMON:** G Sheeran; **H Keegan**, P Doorey, F Nicholson; P Hickey, G Fitzmaurice, D Murray; S Killoran, P McNeill (0-1); E McManus Jnr, J Kelly (0-1), E McManus Snr; T Óg O'Brien (0-2), P Earley (1-0), A Garvey (0-1). **Subs:** J Newton for Kelly, P Gaynor for Keegan.

##

I FIRST STARTED kicking a football around when I was in national school in Tarmon, which was a rural school outside Castlerea. To this day, I still remember my first introduction to organised Gaelic football. The local postman was Danny Burke, a man who has been involved with Roscommon teams for many years.

One day, he pulled up on his bicycle while we were kicking ball and asked if I'd go and train with the Castlerea under-15s. This would have been around 1965 or '66, when Tarmon had no juvenile team and there was talk of amalgamating the two teams. Danny was in charge of the team that year and we ended up winning the under-15 county title.

That was the start of a very good club career with Castlerea, and I would go on to win county titles at minor, under-21 and senior level between 1966 and '71. I won everything there was to win in Roscommon with Castlerea.

THE ACTION

★★★★★

PRETTY MUCH EVERYTHING that could go wrong for Roscommon on July 13, 1986, did go wrong. Coming into this final, the Rossies were without the electric attacking talents of Tony McManus, as well as the sure-footedness of Gary Wynne from their defence. It was perhaps no surprise then that this Connacht showcase was decided on what could be described as yet another moment of sheer bad luck three minutes from time.

The Galway selectors, however, do deserve some credit for the way in which this match concluded. As Roscommon defensive colossus Harry Keegan limped from the field, Stephen Joyce was sprung from the bench with just three minutes remaining. In Keegan's significant absence, and with confusion reigning in the Roscommon ranks, Joyce plundered a late goal for the Tribesmen to turn this low-quality final on its head. Sheeran had done his best to keep Joyce's initial effort out, but the Galway forward managed to raise a green flag at the second attempt.

If ever there was a game for the defensive purists, then this was it. Keegan, who would win a third All Star that year, was the standout player on a day when top-class football was at a premium. Had Tony McManus played, perhaps Roscommon's lead would have been more decisive when Joyce struck for his goal. But Galway were crowned Connacht champions on a day when Lady Luck seemed to have deserted the hosts at Dr Hyde Park.

★★★★★

Following a successful year in 1971, when Castlerea won its third senior title in four years, I was called into the Roscommon senior set-up ahead of the league campaign. My county debut was one to remember, because it was in Nowlan Park against Kilkenny of all teams! John Kerrane, another Castlerea man, had just come back from New York and was playing in that game too. Kilkenny didn't really waste time with the niceties of football. They seemed to enjoy putting themselves about... with or without the hurls!

They had some good footballers too but, as far as I remember, we won that game fairly comfortably. If we hadn't, I'm not sure some of us would have been asked back! I can't remember what division of the league we were in, but it must have been fairly far down the pecking order if we were playing football in Nowlan Park.

I was blessed throughout my time with Roscommon that I had very few injuries. My biggest injury happened against Kerry in 1972 in an All-Ireland semi-final. I was marking Mick O'Dwyer, and I think he was nearly old enough to be my father! He must have been around 36 by then, and I was only 20. I hurt my ankle in that game but didn't have any other injuries for a while after that.

I've broken an arm and a thumb, but my biggest problem as my career went on were my hamstrings. Back then, we didn't have the knowledge of how bad the tear was, so I'd be going around with a big bandage on my thigh just trying to get through a game.

It was a hamstring injury that put me out of the league final against Cork in 1979. That's a game I would have liked to have been part of, but Seamus Tighe came in and did a good job and we beat Cork pretty comfortably anyway.

My first Connacht title arrived in 1972, and it took me five years to win another one. The team was a work in progress between 1972 and '77. We were building something though and there were some good young players coming through. By 1977, we had assembled some fine players and won another Connacht title, but were beaten by Armagh in the All-Ireland semi-final after a replay. Mickey Freyne had a goal disallowed for a square ball, which Paddy Collins the referee later admitted was probably the wrong decision.

More Connacht titles were to come in the following three years but, unfortunately, we just couldn't get over the line in the All-Ireland. Kerry beat us in the semi-final in 1978, and Dublin beat us by a point at the same stage in '79. In 1980, we finally got the semi-final monkey off our backs by beating a good Armagh team. Then we had a final against Kerry and the rest, as they say, is history.

Losing to Kerry is a big regret. I think we held them scoreless for the first 25 minutes and we had even opened up a five-point lead. They came back into it after that, and I think at the end of the game they were just more experienced at seeing out a match. I suppose we had also started to tire a bit… mentally you get tired when a team is constantly coming at you. It's like it gets into your legs through your head! We had opportunities in that game, but we didn't take them and that's where you live and die in football.

I won my second All Star that year, having won my first one two years previously. All Stars are individual awards… it would be alright if you were playing golf, I suppose, but football is a team game. You'd always want to win an All-Ireland… think about what it would mean to those 21 guys and management… think about what it would mean for the county!

At that time, Roscommon had a following that was second to none. I was living in Dublin, but I had people who would drive me down to county training. People like Chris Giblin and Cyril O'Neill. We used to meet the manager, Tom Heneghan in Mullingar on our way down. The drive was colossal back then. There was no motorway, it was mostly back roads. We were very lucky that none of us ever had an accident with all that travelling. Driving back on your own was hard going too. I often left Roscommon after getting a bite to eat in The Royal or The Abbey and you'd be driving through Ballymun at one o'clock in the morning. I remember coming across a Garda checkpoint one night.

'Where ya comin' from?'

Some of them wouldn't believe you when you told them!

Then there was the difficulty of travelling up and down during the petrol shortage in the 1970s. At the time, it was nearly impossible to get petrol in Dublin, so I'd make calls to one or two places that were owned by Roscommon people, just to make sure I'd be able to get a full tank to get me back for work! There was no skitting around Dublin back then because you needed the car for training.

I remember I didn't get down for the celebrations after the 1979 league final because I was afraid I wouldn't get enough petrol to get back for work! My colleagues had given me a lot of support in covering my shifts for different matches, so it was very important that I was there to return the favour. I just couldn't take the chance, despite it being our first national title as a team.

I worked as a psychiatric nurse, and I was lucky to have tremendous colleagues who'd work for me and allow me time off to go and play matches. I must say the management and staff were great. It was tough because I'd have to be back in Dublin to be on the ward at seven o'clock the following morning. Five hours' sleep… and back to work. Luckily, I liked the work, and I liked training… but I loved the buzz of the games!

Living and working in Dublin, I was removed from the build-up to big matches and much of the hype around the team. There wasn't the same pressure on me that the lads who were at home all the time experienced. I'd say their heads were buzzing with people talking to them about some of those games!

The injury I sustained in the 1986 Connacht final at Dr Hyde Park could have been avoided. The damage was done when my foot went into a hole in the pitch. I remember telling someone earlier on when we were training that there was a hole on the right-hand side of the pitch, and asking them to put a bit of sand or clay into it. I thought I was doing well until I was forced off injured, and Stephen Joyce, who had come on with 67 minutes played, got in for the winning goal as I watched on from the sideline.

I couldn't really believe it when I was awarded my third All Star later that year, after going off injured and being beaten in a Connacht final. I often told people, 'Jesus, there must have been an awful scarcity of corner-backs in 1986!' It was nice to win it but again, we lost as a team in a Connacht final.

I think that tactically we failed when it came to replacing me that day. We probably should have brought in a fresh corner-back. I could be wrong, but I'm nearly certain we brought Padraig McNeill out of midfield and into the corner. He used to play a bit alright for the Roscommon Gaels in defence, but I think we needed a fresh man in and one who was a regular corner-back.

A corner-back or full-back at that time couldn't really play anywhere else. It was a specialist position and we had one or two lads on the sideline who were good enough to come in. Look, there's no point in thinking about it now… no one was to blame really. Decisions are made on the day, and you live or die by them.

That was one game that got away because I think we had the beating of

Galway. There were good performances all over the field that day. It was a shame because the team that year was only really getting over our defeat to Sligo in the 1981 semi-final, believe it or not! That was such a bad loss, and I don't think we ever really recovered coming up to 1986. The team was playing well by then and we had some good new lads in. Galway beating us was a bit of a sickener.

The fact that it was Stephen Joyce with the winning goal was hard to take also. Now, he might have got the better of me anyway. I might have got tired or lost concentration for a second, and you'd be sure a poacher like Stephen would be in like a shot. I remember marking the likes of John Tobin and Jimmy Burke and, just like Joyce, you couldn't take your eyes off them for a second. So even if I was on the pitch, there was always a chance that he would have found a way past.

When the end of my Roscommon career arrived it wasn't a case of a light-bulb going off in my head or anything like that. I just wasn't picked!

It was a Connacht semi-final in 1988, and I suppose I was a bit disappointed and annoyed. It wouldn't be natural if you weren't. I felt I still had one big game left in me. I was having injury problems though and so I could see it from the selectors' point of view, whether it was worth taking a chance. Our kids had started to come along too, and it was gradually dawning on me that I wasn't going to be able to hold on to the jersey.

I was lucky that I had never lost my place down through the years. I might have been out injured, but I'd always get back in. We had some very good corner-backs who replaced me at different times. In another era they would have held on to the position.

When the end came, it was quick. I remember sitting in the car with my wife, Margaret on the way back to the hotel. I turned to her and said, 'I'm out!' She didn't say do or don't retire, just, 'Do what you have to do'.

She would have been a great support down through the years and prior to our first child in 1982, would have been at many of the games. But when the babies come along your whole focus starts to change. I was around 36 at that stage… and Jesus I'd been at it for 16 or 17 years!

I had transferred to Fingallians in Swords in 1980, where I was involved in championship and top-class Division One matches in the Dublin leagues. I was up against some of the top Dublin lads at the time too. I played with Kieran Duff in those years.

You were all the time training, maintaining your fitness, and watching your diet. Sometimes you'd miss events and weddings and things like that. I remember leaving a wedding early one Saturday because I had to get to Ruislip to play London… and 16 years is a long time to be making those sacrifices.

I also trained a lot with the football team in St Ita's Hospital, where I worked. We used to play in the inter-hospital competitions. The likes of Ballinasloe, Killarney, Castlebar… they all had football teams and we had a pretty good one out in Portrane. It was 13-a-side league and championship.

I took the training sessions, and we had a few lads from different counties. Very few of them were county players but they loved the training. There was nowhere else to go anyway… there were only two or three buses a day into Portrane, and the pay wasn't great. You were either out with a football or a hurl to pass the time.

I also played a lot of soccer with St Ita's at the time too, so I always fit. When I was in Castlerea I used to play with Castlerea Celtic. The funny thing about that was Mickey Freyne was a forward for Roscommon and I was in the backs, but when we played soccer, I was up front, and he was in the backs! Mickey Freyne, now there was a tremendous player. He won the first All Star for Roscommon in 1972. He played as a roving full-forward, but you'd often find him down beside you in the back line… he was way ahead of his time. If he was playing now, he'd fit into any team because he could get up and down the pitch so easily.

I have no regrets about my Roscommon career. I was one of the lucky ones to get onto those great teams. I wasn't the most skilful of players, but like the rowers from Skibbereen would say… I trained like a dog! Whatever I lacked in skill I made up for through determination. I wasn't a lad for drinking or anything like that, though I did enjoy a few pints after a game. It was a case of looking after myself and making sure I was able to give 100 percent. They were great years, and I met a lot of great people while playing for Roscommon.

We had some bad years too, but you have to have the ups as well as the downs if you're to achieve anything in life. I enjoyed it and I would never regret the sacrifices involved or even those bad days, because it all boiled down to pulling that Primrose and Blue jersey over your head and representing the people of Roscommon.

99

DEREK THOMPSON

ST MEL'S COLLEGE 3-6 ★ GORMANSTON 1-11
Leinster Colleges Semi-Final
Rathkenny, Co Meath
MARCH 12, 1989

★ **ST MEL'S COLLEGE:** D Thompson; T Tighe, C Caslain, P Walsh; P Kelly (0-1), M Trautt, D Ryan; C McGlynn, N Loftus; P Leavy (1-3), T McGuinness (0-1), B Guckian; P Neary (1-1), A Maxwell, G Fay (1-0).

★ **GORMANSTON:** N Monaghan; E McNally, C Murphy, M Shanley; P McCarthy, D Reynolds, H Tully; R Mannion (0-2), P Carolan; M McKenna (0-1), R Delves, C Kelly; P McCaffrey (1-2), N Finnegan, (0-6), N Henry. **Sub:** G McCullough for Shanley.

❝

I HAD PLAYED outfield right up to minors and had no county experience at under-16 or minor level. I did my Inter-Cert in CBS Roscommon and after that I switched schools and went to St Mel's in Longford. I didn't go for try-outs with the school football team right away. Mel's were coming off the back of winning an All-Ireland in 1987, and Ray McMahon was the goalkeeper in '88. They were beaten in the All-Ireland final by St Colman's College, Newry that year.

It was in my Leaving Cert year that I was beginning to play in goals for St Faithleach's at minor level, and so then I decided to go for the goalkeeper's position in Mel's rather than play outfield. I even managed to nail down the 'keeper's jersey for the league campaign and we were motoring along nicely. We went on to win a Leinster league title that year, beating Moyne Community School in the final. Expectations were high once again going into the Leinster Colleges Championship.

THE ACTION

★★★★★

IT'S FAIR TO say, Franciscan College, Gormanston had every right to feel aggrieved at the full-time whistle at Rathkenny on Sunday, March 12, 1989! St Mel's, with the future Roscommon senior goalkeeper, Derek Thompson in goals, were going for a hat-trick of Leinster titles, but that bid should probably have come unstuck here.

Niall Finnegan and Peadar McCaffrey, alongside Robert Delves, had led the champions' defence on a merry dance in the first-half, helping the Meath college into a three-point interval lead, 1-7 to 1-4. The torment showed no signs of letting up for Mel's after the break either, and but for McCaffrey's forced withdrawal into defence, Gormanston looked certain to advance to the final.

As it was, they held a seemingly unassailable 1-10 to 1-5 lead with normal time almost up. Then, drama, as Paul Neary found the net, and Paddy Kelly split the posts. A lifeline for St Mel's title defence, that was, until Ralph Mannion's point appeared to have finally made the game safe for Gormanston.

Incredibly, there was still time for one final dramatic act. A peach of a pass from Alan Maxwell ripped through the Meath school's defence and into the grateful arms of Gearoid Fay, who was left with the easy task of blasting the ball to the Gormanston net and keeping Mel's' hopes of a Leinster hat-trick alive!

★★★★★

The late 80s was a period of dominance for St Mel's, not seen since the 1930s and 40s. Looking back on those days, it's hard to believe the school has only won two Leinster titles in the last 33 years. It just seemed like the glory years would go on forever in 1988-89. We were comfortable in the championship that year and made it to the semi-final stage without too much fuss.

Our main rivals at that time would have been Moyne and Moate. Coming into the Leinster Championship you would have been looking at St Pat's in Navan and St Peter's in Wexford.

We went into the semi-final against Gormanston, without any real fear. Fr Peter Burke was our manager at the time, and he was absolutely brilliant – right there in the top three trainers I've ever played under. We trained up in the 'Bishop's field' and it was just that... a field with portable goals. Fr Burke's attitude was, 'If they can run in the muck, when the grass comes in spring-time, they'll be flying it'.

There was no goalkeeping coach in those days, so I was stuck running in the muck with everyone else!

St Mel's was the kind of place where the 'boarders' were brought out to what we called the smoking sheds, where they'd go through an hour of practicing their chants and songs for matches. The whole experience was a world away from playing minors at St Faithleach's, especially when it came to the Leinster Championship matches!

Four or five busloads of students would be shipped to wherever we were playing and they'd spend the match chanting and cheering us on. It was alien to us lads who were used to club football. I was playing alongside lads who had plenty of county under-16 experience with the likes of Leitrim and Longford, and we also had Paddy Kelly from Roscommon. But even the lads playing Ted Webb football wouldn't have been used to an atmosphere like that!

In the build-up to the match against Gormanston, Peter Burke brought us into the conference room in Mel's for a tactical talk. You could tell by him that he didn't think we were going to coast through this one.

'These Gormanston lads are different to what ye've played,' he said.

'They don't have it here!' he said, circling his hand on his stomach. 'But... up here, they think they're excellent,' he added, tapping his head. He was expecting a difficult game and he was trying to prepare us for it while also giving us something to cling to in terms of Gormanston's weaknesses.

I remember the game was played in Rathkenny in County Meath, a place I don't think any of us had ever heard of before. True to what Burke had said, the game was very tight… until we found ourselves five points down going into second-half injury-time!

Much like the Connacht final of 2001, games like that Leinster Colleges semi-final, when you win at the very death, always stand out. There's usually a big prize for winning those games too, whether it's a trophy or a place in a final.

At five points down, it looked all over, but as champions often do, we somehow found a way back from the dead. Paul Neary got in for a goal, and then we got a point. But when they responded with a point of their own, it looked like our hopes were dashed once more. It was a mad finish to a match!

A clubmate of mine, Mel Trautt, was playing centre-back in that match. I'll never forget what happened next because it cemented my decision to play in goals for the rest of my career!

The pitch was on a bit of a slope and Gormanston were playing 'downhill' in that second-half. The game was deep in injury-time, when the ball was kicked down our end of the field. At that moment, Mel seemed to lose his footing and, suddenly, I had had three Gormanston forwards bearing down on me…

The smart thing would have been to draw me out and leave a teammate with an easy fisted goal, but a rasping shot came in and it was just a pure reaction save… getting my fingertips to it and diverting it away from the top corner of the net. What a feeling, and I was officially HOOKED on goalkeeping!

We launched one more attack after that, and Alan Maxwell managed to find Gearoid Fay with a superb pass. It was an easy chance for Fay, and he made no mistake, finishing to the net to complete our comeback.

What stands out most from that game is what happened afterwards. My late dad and uncle, John Kenny were at the game. When they tried to jump the fence to get out onto the field, John lost his glasses. It was good job he managed to keep them on for injury-time or he might have been congratulating the Gormanston lads instead!

I'll never forget my dad out on the pitch afterwards… he looked so proud. That image of him there has always stuck with me throughout the years.

While dad and John had made it out onto the pitch, it became obvious very soon after the final whistle that some of our supporters were missing. It turned out that they had got back on the bus and headed off to school, thinking the game was lost. So much for all their practice in the smoking sheds!

We actually stopped off in Mullingar on the way home for some chicken and chips, and met some supporters there. There were no smartphones or even mobile phones in those days. I think they had to go out to their cars or to the buses to listen to the news, because they still couldn't believe we'd won the game!

We went on to win the Leinster Colleges title that year against Moyle Park from Clondalkin, a team which featured a certain Jim Gavin at centre half-forward. It's fair to say that Leinster title was won in Rathkenny, however, as the final was a far more straightforward win. We hammered the Dublin school, 1-16 to 0-3.

Sadly, we didn't manage to win an All-Ireland. Colin Corkery and Coláiste Chríost Rí beat us in the semi-final before going on to lose the final to St Patrick's College, Maghera.

The game against Gormanston was definitely our toughest game all year. That last-minute save was made even more satisfying by the fact that it kept us in it at the end and afforded us one last chance to grab a winner. The game was special not just because of the manner of our victory, but also because it helped me to find my permanent position on the field. It's safe to say I fell in love with goalkeeping that day.

At club level, Mark Crehan was our goalkeeper, but I remember the goalmouths at St Faithleach's were in bits around that time. They were just muck and water, and I think Mark had grown tired of diving around in them.

'Let me have a go at it'. Of course, it helped that I had a bit of a grá for it too, otherwise goals can be a very lonely position! There's no doubt though that nailing down the number one spot at Mel's for league and championship, and making some great saves in that Leinster semi-final, had me thinking it was a great position to play in.

Now, obviously if you fast-forward to the Connacht final against Galway in 1998, you see the other side of it. When you drop the ball in a big game with thousands of people watching on, it's certainly not the best place to be! But it was great walking off the pitch that day in Rathkenny and receiving the pats on the back that are usually reserved for forwards.

The late save and my performance overall won me the *Longford Sports Star of the Month*. It was the *Longford Leader* who used to give out the award and I remember it was Benny O'Brien who presented it to me.

Following that Leinster Colleges win for St Mel's, I soon got a call from Pat Lindsay to go into the Roscommon under-21 set-up. Dermot Earley then called me up to the senior panel after winning the county intermediate title with St Faithleach's in 1992 under Kevin McStay. Things were happening quickly for me in those years.

After playing well with Mel's and the Roscommon under-21s, I was still young enough when I took over the goalkeeper's jersey at Faithleach's, but the confidence was there However, just like that transition from St Faithleach's minors to championship with St Mel's, moving from intermediate football to the Roscommon senior panel is a big step up. Playing in goals, you are probably more nervous too. You're the last line of defence so you just can't afford to make any mistakes. Playing outfield, if you make a mistake there's always someone who will get you out of trouble, but not so when you're between the posts.

I found that those thoughts of making a mistake would play on my mind a bit in the build-up to big matches. Then it changes when the game begins and you're too busy concentrating to really think about anything else. When Roscommon won the Connacht title in 2001, one of the standout moments for me came against Galway in the semi-final in Tuam Stadium. I remember bawling my eyes out after that one...the RELIEF! It was a mixture of everything really... that mistake in '98, finally beating Galway, and making it to another Connacht final. It was just a huge weight off my shoulders.

Further back, I remember my first ever Connacht Championship game. It was against Sligo at the Hyde. Afterwards we were allowed go to The Royal Hotel for a pint... but I don't think I could even manage one that night. The nervous energy had me completely zapped! It all started in the lead up to a game for me.

You're stressing out the few days before, but you don't even realise it. I suppose you do have to be a bit mad to be a goalkeeper!

The great thing about Gaelic football – whatever level you play at – is the amazing people you meet along the way. Recently, I was at the Hyde for a league game between Roscommon and Donegal, and I pulled into the local petrol station to fill up. I was standing at the car and a man came out of the shop, and made a beeline towards me.

He leaned on the roof of my car and looked straight at me.

'Bet you don't know who I am?'

'I actually do know ya!' I shot back, 'Now, don't say anything else!'

I reached into my pocket and pulled my Garda badge out. Behind the photograph there was a four-leafed clover. The man leaning on the roof of my car had given it to me in 2001 in Tuam Stadium. I had gone to retrieve the ball behind the goal at one stage and he grabbed my hand through the wire, pressing this little card into it.

'Ye'll win it now today!'

And we did.

I had kept that little clover in my glove all through my years in goal for Roscommon. It certainly brought me plenty of luck, particularly in Tuam Stadium and Dr Hyde Park in 2001.

It was a lovely moment outside the Hyde that day when all those years playing for Roscommon came full circle.

SEAMUS KILLORAN

ROSCOMMON 0-16 ★ GALWAY 1-11
Connacht SFC Final
Dr Hyde Park
JULY 22, 1990

★ **ROSCOMMON:** P Staunton; G Wynne, P Doorey, D Newton; J Connaughton, D Brady, P Hickey; **S Killoran**, J Newton (0-1); T Grehan (0-1), E McManus (0-5), A Leyland (0-1); T Lennon (0-2), P Earley (0-4), T McManus (0-1). **Subs:** V Glennon (0-1) for Grehan, P McNeill for Leyland.

★ **GALWAY:** P Comer; B Silke, G O'Farrell, F McWalter; J Fallon (0-2), A Mulholland, A O'Shea; B Moylan, H Bleahen; C O'Dea, V Daly (0-8), T Mannion (0-1); T Kilcommins, D Croucher, F O'Neill (1-0). **Subs:** P Fallon for Silke, P O'Dea for Croucher, B Barrett for C O'Dea.

THE DISAPPOINTMENT OF losing the 1989 Connacht final to Mayo was still a big thing for us going into the following year. We felt like we had let that game slip because we knew we were every bit as good as Mayo. They went on to basically give away an All-Ireland that year to Cork. We were still hurt over that. There was only a kick of a ball in it, really. It could have gone our way and maybe it should have gone our way too.

We were promoted in the league that year after losing just one match in Division Two. We were trying to build something and hoping that we'd at least do as well as the previous year and reach the final again. There was definitely a feeling that we did need to get across the line, because our team had been around for a while knocking on the door. Time was moving on and we knew we had to grab our opportunity.

THE ACTION

★★★★★

THE TRIBESMEN WERE strong favourites to seal yet another provincial title following their victory over Mayo in the semi-final. The game itself was a slow burner, but when it did finally come to life both sides played some great football, particularly in the second-half. Tommy Lennon had given Roscommon an early lead before Galway roared into life with Val Daly leading from the front. Roscommon did improve as the first-half wore on and points from the impressive Eamonn Junior McManus, Paul Earley and Andy Leyland sent the sides in level at the break at six points apiece.

The second-half provided much better viewing for the spectators as Roscommon came flying out of the blocks with scores from Tommy Lennon, John Newton and Tommy Grehan.

McManus kicked two terrific points from long range, and Roscommon suddenly led by 0–13 to 0–8 with just 15 minutes remaining. However, with Daly in top form, Galway were far from beaten and a massive Daly point from all of 50 metres out gave the travelling supporters hope. If a late Fergal O'Neill goal, laid on for him by that man Daly, had the hosts chewing their fingernails, then another inspirational Daly point just a minute later must have had them chewing their fingers!

Just as the Roscommon supporters began to fear the worst, however, up stepped that man again Eamonn McManus, and another superb point from the Clann marksman sealed a well-deserved and long-awaited Connacht final win for the Primrose and Blue.

★★★★★

We scored five goals against London in our quarter-final in Ruislip and then edged past Leitrim in the semi-final. The final was at Hyde Park against Galway. Roscommon traditionally play well against Galway. We always felt we had a chance anyway because we had built them up in our own heads as cocky. We always told ourselves that they felt entitled to win! When it comes to games against Mayo, you'd nearly feel you had to be on top of your game to have any chance... but Galway were a different story. Maybe it was something to do with the style of football both teams played.

1990 wasn't the best for me personally. I lost my father that year. I remember going up to Ballinasloe Hospital the day before the Connacht final to see him. I was told one of the girls nursing my father was a sister of one of the Galway players I'd be facing the next day. Who she was I still don't know, and it probably went over my head at the time because my father was so sick. He had been ill with cancer for quite a while. He died in September of that year.

My father had very little interest in football, but that was neither here nor there to me. I would have to give my mother credit for my interest in the sport. Her first cousin was Harry Connor, who won an All-Ireland with Roscommon in the 1940s. He was one of the older lads at that stage, but played for Roscommon for a long time. So, it's fair to say the football came from that side of the family.

Little did I know, however, that football would become such an important part of my life... just ask my wife, Una! We were married the following year, in 1991, just two days before the Connacht final replay.

My argument to her was, 'I can get married nine months of the year, but you're only available for three months!' She was a schoolteacher, and only retired recently. But we had our dates chosen carefully to work around the football, and the replay didn't affect us. Even the honeymoon was only delayed for two weeks!

There was a lot happening in those two years. I was only in my late 20s and self-employed as a dairy farmer. If you're involved with a team though at a high level, your focus is nearly with the team first and everything else second. If that's not your mindset, then you're probably better off at home because you'll soon be found out. If I got up in the morning and knew I had to be in Kiltoom for eight o'clock that evening, I'd be trying to organise my day to make sure I was there. That's the way it was.

The most important thing about the Connacht final that year was that we won it! Playing good football is nice, but it's not much consolation if you play well and you get beaten. You've a job to do and as soon as that ball is thrown in it's up to you to come out on top in your own contest to help your team. You do need a bit of luck at times too...

John Newton and myself complemented each other well at midfield. Sometimes it can be hard enough to get one player around there who's fairly handy, but we worked very well together as a partnership. In that era, there were far more contests across the pitch. The ball went in and two, three and even four players fought for it, whereas now that doesn't happen. It's more of a running game nowadays.

I enjoyed those contests and loved going up against the likes of Liam McHale from Mayo or Kerry's Jack O'Shea, another brilliant footballer and a tough man. I remember Jack running into me one year in Tralee and breaking his nose! It was just unfortunate the way it happened. He turned into me and lifted his head at the wrong moment. Jack was a grand fella. The next time I met him was when I was playing for Connacht in the Railway Cup. I asked him how his nose was, and he shook hands with me and laughed. The Kerry supporters weren't quite so forgiving the day it happened, however.

We used to take the Fridays off before the very big games to prepare tactically. This was on top of our normal training. We had a right good group of lads, and the spirit was excellent in the team. There was a fair bit of talent and a lot of drive too. That's why 1989 was such a disappointment. We were ahead at the right time, but we didn't look after one kickout and that was that. I suppose it comes down to someone making a mistake or not doing their job correctly... look, the spectators or the media can blame fellas, but we are just volunteers at the end of the day, doing something we enjoy.

Marty McDermott was the manager that year, and we had John Kelly from Boyle and Sean Kilbride from Kiltoom as selectors. Joe Mulligan did the physical training. I think he was a PE teacher based in Athlone at the time. His brother was an All-Ireland winner with Offaly. Joe was fairly modern, maybe a year or two ahead of his time. Marty was forward thinking too and even brought a sports psychologist into us at one stage. I didn't really buy into a lot of that sort of stuff. One thing that never changes about football or any sport is that you have to be committed and put in one hundred percent effort. If you don't do that, then you're going to be on the hind foot and no amount of psychology will help you.

There was a three or four-year period during my time with Roscommon where we didn't expect to lose a game. It would come down to maybe a bad refereeing decision, a missed free, or not taking a great goal chance. For a time, that was really the only difference, whether we won or lost. It didn't matter who we were playing. We were in around the third or fourth best team in the country during those years. An exceptional group of players. We thought anything was possible.

The one thing I remember quite clearly about that 1990 Connacht final was Val Daly. He played very well that day. He used to nick in front of his marker and score points for fun. My mind-set for every game was just to work hard, fight for every ball and try and help my teammates. I was one of these players who flew under the radar. I certainly wasn't a man for the media or anything like that. I was only interested in getting out and playing the game. Our star man that day was Eamonn Junior McManus. He scored five points and ran the show. Paul Earley was good too and so too were our backs. We got on top at midfield and John Newton even ventured forward and scored a point.

The final was tight all the way through, and I had a chance or two to wrap it up near the end, but it didn't go at all well! I was never a finisher, in fairness. Thankfully, we managed to hang in there until the final whistle and I didn't have to worry about squandering my chance.

In terms of the celebrations after, well we just felt privileged to be part of it all. You couldn't help but think back to 1989 and the fact that you missed out on it. It made me appreciate 1990 more. I think we went up the town and did a bit of a tour around the county. It was certainly much nicer winning a Connacht final than losing one!

It was unfortunate that our championship came to an end in the very next match against the reigning All-Ireland champions Cork. They were very good in that semi-final against us and would go on to win the All-Ireland that year. You could debate that we just weren't good enough. I was always of the feeling that we needed to get out of Connacht in 1989. If we'd done that, then in 1990 we would have had a much better chance.

We were slightly unfortunate in that Cork game too, it must be said. We were playing well in the first-half but then Padraig McNeill and I were both injured. McNeill was concussed and I injured my shoulder… so we lost our centre half-back and one of our two midfielders. I think they scored four or five points in the last few minutes. That put a bigger gap between us on the scoreboard than we probably deserved.

The following year we lost to Meath in the semi-final. We were six points up with 15 minutes to go, and they came back and won. We beat ourselves that year. We panicked a bit, instead of playing it simple and making 20-yard passes and being more careful with the ball. These are the small things that decide if you win or not. It's about making the right decision at the right time. You can do all the training you want and work on something a hundred times, but unless you're able to do it when the pressure is on, it's no good.

I enjoyed playing at Croke Park. At that time, Roscommon rarely got to play there, whereas now you can nearly head up for the craic! There was no back door in those days either. You were there for a semi-final or final; there were no Mickey Mouse games then. If you played a league game against Dublin it was nearly unheard of to be playing in Croke Park. For that reason, Croke Park was held up as a special venue. It was a great honour to play there for Roscommon, particularly when you're from a rural club like I was.

I am proud of my time with the county team. I played for Roscommon for 10 years or so and was nearly always in the team. I had a few injuries, but nothing too bad… although there might still be a few sore spots now! Playing for Roscommon brought me all over the country and I met the finest of people. I played with and against great lads too. If I could do it all again… I suppose the only change I'd make is winning an All-Ireland, and maybe throw in another Connacht title or two.

Above all else, Gaelic football was a bit of a release for me from my daily routine. When you work in farming, you can be left isolated sometimes. Then suddenly, you're a county footballer and you're all over the place and surrounded by people. I remember when I was first called up to the senior panel and had to go up to Roscommon. I wasn't impressed. 'I'm not going to f***** stick this. It's a long drive up there,' I said.

I was used to tipping five minutes up the road to Elphin for training from underage. I left school early and then didn't play football for 18 months. I was on the farm one evening and the local insurance broker, Joe Brady, the Lord be good to him, called out to see if I'd play a minor game for the club because they'd only 14 players. This was before mobile phones and all that. I rummaged around for a pair of boots and went up. I think we lost to a Kilmore-Shannon Gaels amalgamation, which featured John Newton. But it got me back into football at least.

Life works in funny ways. If Elphin had 15 players that day or Joe Brady didn't arrive out to the house... you just never know. One thing's for sure, if it's for you, it won't pass you by. I'm glad the opportunity to play for Roscommon didn't pass me by.

"

JOHN NEWTON
(& ENON GAVIN)

ROSCOMMON 0-13 ★ MAYO 1-9
Connacht SFC Final Replay
Dr Hyde Park, Roscommon
JULY 28, 1991

★ **ROSCOMMON:** G Sheeran; D Newton, P Doorey, **E Gavin**; J Connaughton, P Hickey, M Reilly; S Killoran, **J Newton (0-1)**; T Grehan (0-1), T McManus (0-1), V Glennon; M Donlon (0-2), P Earley, D Duggan (0-8). **Sub:** E McManus Jnr for Donlon.

★ **MAYO:** E Lavin; A McGarry, P Ford, D Flanagan; P Butler, T Tierney (0-1), J Finn; TJ Kilgallon, C McManamon (0-1); P McStay (0-2), L McHale (0-1), N Durkin; M Fitzmaurice (0-3), T Morley, R Dempsey. **Subs:** WJ Padden (0-1) for McManamon, A Finnerty (1-0) for Morley.

❝

I WAS IN my late twenties in the summer of 1991 and a Garda stationed in Dublin. This meant I was working three Sundays out of four, so I was playing for the Garda club up there, because it just wasn't feasible to be going up and down to play club football with Shannon Gaels. I was lucky to get time off for county training because with the lack of manpower in the guards now, I don't think I'd get off at all. At that time, the country was full of guards playing county football… I'm not sure I could even name one at this stage.

I was stationed in Dublin for my entire service which meant travelling up and down to play with Roscommon. It wasn't too bad during the winter because the league wasn't taken as seriously as it is now. You could 'winter well', as the man says. As long as you started doing a bit of serious training around April, the management were happy enough.

THE ACTION

★★★★★

ROSCOMMON MADE IT back-to-back Connacht senior titles in 1991 in front of around 24,000 people at a sunny Dr Hyde Park, but it might have been a different story entirely had Derek Duggan's last-gasp long-range free not dug Marty McDermott's charges out of a major hole at MacHale Park just two weeks previously.

As it was, Duggan's red-hot form continued in the replay as the teenager scored 0-8 and proved a thorn in Mayo's side all afternoon.

Roscommon were in the ascendancy from the first whistle at the Hyde and raced into an early four-point lead. It was a first-half performance of real authority and the hosts deservedly led 0-7 to 0-4 at the break.

In fact, Roscommon looked to be relatively in control against their arch rivals right up until the 54th minute, when a controversial Anthony Finnerty goal suddenly thrust Mayo into a two-point lead. Finnerty's shove on Des Newton went unnoticed and the Mayo man took full advantage, blasting the ball past Gay Sheeran in the Roscommon goal.

The Rossies regained their composure. John Newton's move into the forwards gave Roscommon a new attacking dimension and his well-taken improvised point went a long way to steadying the ship. Nineteen-year-old Duggan also kept his cool in front of the posts to ensure the JJ Nestor Cup would be spending yet another winter with the Primrose and Blue.

★★★★★

You'd be on the go three or four days of the week. Down to Roscommon on Saturday during the winter… and then Tuesdays and Thursdays in the Hyde or Kiltoom for championship training later in the year. There would be some type of match most Sundays after the league finished, whether it was a challenge or championship game.

Paul Earley had been captain in 1990, and then Marty McDermott called me and asked me to captain the team the following year. It was a great personal honour at the time and it's something that will always bring me great pride.

Leading Roscommon out for a big match and then getting to lift the Nestor Cup at the Hyde are wonderful memories to look back on. You probably don't pass too much heed on it at the time. You certainly don't wake up on the morning of a match and think about making speeches in front of a packed Hyde or anything like that! But I do look back on 1991 as the pinnacle of my career; things went very well for me that year – in both league and championship.

Roscommon were always known as a physical and dogged team who were hard to beat, but I think we showed we could also play football that day in the Connacht final replay against Mayo. We reached the National League semi-finals in 1991 too, beating Tyrone in the quarter-final before losing to Dublin. We had beaten Dublin the year before after extra-time so we were capable of mixing it with anyone at that stage. I can also remember playing Meath in a league match in Kiltoom around about that time and beating them well. I think that has to go down as the best team display that I was ever involved in.

We came into the Connacht Championship that year as defending champions after beating Galway in the final the year before, and we felt we were building something special at that stage. Between 1990 and '91, we played in four national semi-finals including two National League semi-finals and two All-Ireland semi-finals. We had also played that year's All-Ireland champions Cork in the 1990 league semi-final, and there wasn't much in it. They just pulled away from us with about 10 minutes to go. So, hopes were reasonably high going into the 1991 championship.

Our first match was against Leitrim in the semi-final that year. They had hammered Sligo in the quarter-final to set up a home game against us at Pairc Sean Mac Diarmada. Shannon Gaels are based near Carrick-on-Shannon and so there would be a big rivalry with Leitrim. They would come through three years later and win a Connacht title, so there's no doubt they had a good team in the early 90s. They were already very competitive in 1991 so that was a game we had to take seriously. It wasn't exactly a classic either, but we did just enough to qualify for the final, beating our neighbours by four points in the end.

Our reward was a Connacht final against Mayo at MacHale Park in Castlebar. Mayo had hit serious form that summer, after putting six goals past London in the opening round at Ruislip. They were equally as impressive against Galway in their semi-final, beating the Tribesmen 3-11 to 0-6. We may have been reigning champions but on form, Mayo, who were All-Ireland finalists just two years earlier, would have been very confident playing us on their home turf.

They had every reason to be confident as we were forced to rally against the wind in the second-half. It looked like Liam McHale had won it for them very late on, before Derek Duggan equalised with his famous free with nearly the last kick of the game. That rescued a replay for us at the Hyde two weeks later.

The first thing I remember about the replay was that the weather could not have been more different. It had been a wet and miserable day in Castlebar the first day, but July 28 was warm and sunny. We trained well in the couple of weeks between both games and started the match brilliantly, racing into a 0-5 to 0-2 lead. We maintained that until half-time, and 10 minutes into the second-half we found ourselves four points clear.

Midfield was one of Mayo's strongest sectors but we more than held our own for most of the match against the likes of Liam McHale, TJ Kilgallon and Colm McManamon. It was all going according to plan really, until Willie Joe Padden came on and kicked the ball over the bar from about 60 yards to spark a Mayo revival.

Then disaster… A high ball came in on our full-back line and it was Anthony Finnerty who reacted quickest, grabbing the ball and crashing it into our net. It was a bit of a dubious goal because it looked like Finnerty had pushed Des in the back just before scoring. The referee did run to the umpires to check it, but the goal stood, and Mayo were suddenly back in it. With our four-point cushion suddenly gone, the game was nip and tuck from Finnerty's goal right to the end.

It looked at one stage as if the momentum was completely shifting in Mayo's favour when they managed to go ahead late on. This prompted our management to move me in to full-forward with about 10 minutes to go in order to give us more options in attack. It seemed to do the trick, and I kicked the equaliser with the outside of my right boot before we won a free in injury-time. Derek Duggan, the hero of the first day, kicked what proved to be the winning score to spark huge celebrations at the full-time whistle.

We probably should have been a lot more comfortable in the end, and we could easily have been awarded a penalty late on. Myself and Seamus Killoran missed a couple of late chances too. We had adopted a running game that year and it really paid off in the closing stages and put Mayo on the back foot. They couldn't live with the likes of Tony McManus and Vinny Glennon running directly at them, and that's how the winning free came about.

There were around 30,000 people in the Hyde that day and the place was rocking for most of the afternoon. There may have been a few worried faces and some nervous silence for a few minutes towards the end, but Derek's winning point brought everyone onto the pitch at the final whistle!

I was reasonably happy with my own performance, without thinking I had a great game. From what I remember, Mick O'Dwyer was doing co-commentary with Ger Canning for RTÉ, and I was very surprised that he selected me as Man of the Match. I thought I had played way better in Castlebar in the drawn match. Maybe the fact that I'd scored the equalising point and caught a few balls around the middle of the field swung it for me. My midfield partner, Seamus Killoran, used to always give out about our partnership.

'I do the running for the two of us,' he'd say. 'You go up and catch a ball and get all the glory and the headlines… while I'm chasing two midfielders!'

He may have had a point!

As captain, it was an honour to go up and lift the Nestor Cup. It's hard to believe it now but that was the last time the county managed to retain the Connacht title. Of course, we had no idea how long we'd have to wait to win another one back after that warm summer's day in 1991.

I remember looking down over the pitch as I prepared to accept the cup… I couldn't see a patch of green grass, the place was covered with Roscommon supporters, and all in great humour! I saw my father at one stage, a man who wouldn't be prone to showing a lot of emotion… there he was punching the air with both hands. He was never a man to give you too much praise or anything, but I don't think I ever saw him as happy as he was in that moment.

There were great celebrations back in the dressing-room, before Marty McDermott came in and brought us back down to earth. 'Ye have two weeks lads until an All-Ireland semi-final. Enjoy the night… but back to work next week'.

As was the tradition at the time, we went back to the old Royal Hotel for a meal after the match, while I think Mayo were based at The Abbey Hotel. We were there until late in the evening before we headed back to Glancy's in Carrick-on-Shannon. It's a real GAA pub just on the Roscommon side of the bridge. When I arrived back, there were a couple of hundred people outside waiting for us. Suddenly, I was lifted shoulder high with the cup and carried into the bar.

I gave someone the cup to mind while I enjoyed a few pints.

My younger brother, Paul and a couple of his mates decided it would be a good idea to bring the cup up the town to show the Leitrim supporters! I hadn't even realised the cup was gone… until I found it a bit worse for wear the following morning. Luckily, someone had spotted Paul bringing the cup for a tour of Carrick. Seemingly the locals had then taken the cup for their own tour, and it got a small bit beaten up along the way. In the end, I had to bring it into the jewellers to get it back somehow to its original form. That was my abiding memory of that day!

We generally went to Roscommon town on the Monday after championship matches for a good blow out. At that time, The Royal Hotel was in the hands of the O'Gara family and John and Larry told me if there was no one on reception to just take a key off the wall and have a room for the night. I did it that night… and it was well into Tuesday before I got home!

Training resumed on the Wednesday night. Our 'recovery session' involved running the drink of the previous two or three days out of the system. It was a fairly basic recovery programme, but it always did the trick! The All-Ireland semi-final was still three weeks away at that point, but we were eager to turn our minds to it following the great Connacht celebrations.

We prepared well in those weeks, and I don't think we played too badly against Meath that year. It will probably go down as a game we left behind us. From a positive point of view, it will always be remembered for the goal Derek Duggan scored in front of Hill 16, and his total of 1-8.

The plan was usually for me to play midfield and then move into the forwards with about 10 minutes remaining. But things hadn't gone too well for me at midfield that day. It goes back to the Sunday before the semi-final. Marty was supposed to be doing a preview interview for *The Sunday Game*, but he called me and asked me if I'd go in instead.

'Ah… okay so!'

I arrived at RTÉ, and Seán Boylan was there as well. We did our piece with Michael Lyster and I remember chatting to Seán in the carpark afterwards. He was a fella I had great time for.

'Jezz, you're having a great year. I don't know what we'll do with you next Sunday'.

But, obviously, the wily Seán had hatched a plan! I was marking Liam Hayes the following Sunday, but Colm Coyle was playing wing-forward, and he came across and stood in front of me the whole game. I just couldn't get a run on the ball. He'd dart out in front of my runs every time I tried to go up for it. I was punching him in the back, kneeing him in the hamstrings, but he just wouldn't go away. He was one of these terrier-type footballers and you'd nearly have to kill him to get rid of him! I went in at full-forward anyway with 10 minutes to go and Paul Earley came out to midfield. A switch which had worked wonders in the Connacht final. I remember looking up at the scoreboard with about eight minutes left… and we were five points up at that stage.

I'm going to captain my county in an All-Ireland final…

Win or lose on All-Ireland final day, it would have been a great thing to do. Up to then, our full-back line had played very well. Meath had Colm O'Rourke, Brian Stafford and Bernard Flynn in the forward line. Des and Enon Gavin were keeping O'Rourke and Flynn relatively quiet, but Stafford ended up with nine points that day. He scored six points in-a-row towards the end, and they ended up beating us by a point. That was the end of the line for us that year.

We had a four or five-year spell around that time where you could legitimately say Roscommon were top four in the country. If we had beaten Meath in that semi-final we would have been playing Down in the final. That would have been a 50-50 game, because the Ulster champions weren't really world beaters at that time either. The two traditionally big teams, Kerry and Dublin, weren't at their best so it was a good time to be competing… and it would have been a great time to win an All-Ireland.

★ ★ ★ ★ ★

ENON GAVIN

66

PLAYING FOR CLANN at that time meant I was used to coming up against top forwards during our Connacht and All-Ireland club matches. That was a good thing because I was a late developer as a footballer and never made any of the underage teams for Roscommon. I played a small bit of under-21 in 1991, but I had already made my senior debut by then.

I was picked off the back of Clann's county title wins in 1989, '90 and '91. I consider myself very lucky because I had a really good team around me – one of the best club teams in Ireland at the time. That allowed me to stand out a bit and my more experienced teammates gave me a chance to shine.

My very first game for Roscommon was a league game against Donegal in March of that year. I had been out at my friend's 21st birthday party the night before but I presumed that was okay because I wasn't expecting to get any game time. The next day I went into Roscommon to meet the team… and was told that our corner-back Gary Wynne was unavailable, and I would be starting. Declan Bonner was my marker that day… suddenly, the 21st birthday didn't seem like such a good idea! There were no mobile phones back then, of course, and no Twitter or anything like that. The only way you'd hear about injury concerns for players or the possible starting 15 was at team meetings. I remember my friends were in town after the match and I went in to see them. They couldn't believe it when I told them I had actually been playing.

In my first year with the team, we got to a league semi-final against Dublin. Our form had been mixed enough in the league; we won four and lost three of our seven games. But it was good to get a bit of a run of games and we managed to beat Tyrone in the quarter-final before the Dubs beat us comfortably enough in the last four. I then made my championship debut against Leitrim in a semi-final up in Carrick at the age of 20. They were always tough opposition, but we did enough to get over the line by four points. With respect to Leitrim, we'd be favourites to beat them in most games between the two counties, but it nearly always came down to a tight game, especially at Pairc Seán. I didn't play too badly that day… at least I wasn't given the hook anyway! It was a positive debut, you could say. Derek Duggan was making his first championship appearance as well, and he would go on to have a memorable summer.

At the time, I was working for Elan Pharmaceuticals and living in Athlone, so going back and forth to training wasn't too hard on me. A county like Roscommon would always have lads travelling up and down from places like Dublin and Galway, and I always admired those lads for their massive commitment to the cause.

Back in the early 90s, we were allowed have a few pints after a game… which we did! We had a great night out after the Leitrim game. There were some super nights between those championship games because we had the two or three weeks to recover.

Next up for us was an always daunting fixture… Mayo in Castlebar. It doesn't matter what state or form the Mayo team is in, MacHale Park is always a tough place to go and the games there are usually tight all the way through… or worse!

I could probably be described as a 'sticky marker', and so I could find myself marking two or three different players across the course of 70 minutes. Mayo had some excellent attacking players and from what I remember, I was up against Paul McStay and Maurice Sheridan at various stages. It was dicey enough that day in Castlebar and just when it looked like we'd been beaten, Derek Duggan kicked a monster free to earn us a draw and a replay back in Dr Hyde Park two weeks later.

The training that year might not have been as professional as it now, but we trained just as hard. We ran up f****** mountains, through lakes, bogs… the Carnagh rifle range obstacle courses. There were even psychologists brought in to work with us. It was very new back then and perhaps came a bit too early for some of us…

'Tell me about yourself.'
'I play in the backs.'
'Any concerns?'
'No, not really.'
'Good luck.'

I do remember the media coverage in the build-up to the Connacht final replay, but it certainly wasn't as intense as it is now with all the different newspapers, radio programmes, and also the constant commentary on social media.

The build-up to the final had been huge anyway. I'd played in county finals for Clann but never experienced anything like this. I was still only a kid and a newcomer at the time, but we had the likes of John Newton, Tony McManus, Gay Sheeran, who would have been seven or eight years older. Being so young, you'd have no fear sometimes, but they, on the other hand, were maybe a little bit cagey. They weren't naïve like me; they knew only too well what was at stake. Those older players were so good to me at the time and if there was any bit of rough and tumble during a match, they'd be straight in to help. It was a huge boost knowing your teammates had your back.

A Connacht final at the Hyde was a huge game for a young fella to be involved in. The place was packed that day and you felt there was a lot of pressure on us to perform. There was also nowhere to hide when you were marking man for man. If you went for a ball and missed it and your man got in behind the full-back line, it could be game over. As a back, if there were 10 balls kicked in, you had to win the 10 of them.

That just doesn't happen, no matter how good you are. The forwards of course have it a bit easier! All my man had to do was win one ball… and stick it in the back of the net. Then the headline was… 'ENON GAVIN NIGHTMARE!'

The second day was every bit as tough as the first. We had learned a lot about each other in Castlebar so there were different tactics used in the replay, with both sides trying to find an edge. I was switched into centre-back for a while and that's where Willie Joe Padden was operating when he came on for Mayo with around 37 minutes played. That was a tough battle. He was a household name at the time, while I was only a scruffy gassun!

I don't remember much in terms of my overall performance. I'd nearly need to watch it back! My job was to keep my marker out of the game, and I managed to do that as much as possible. I was a physical player, but you had to be if you wanted to get out in front and keep the ball away from those dangerous forwards. If my man didn't touch the ball, then I knew I'd done my job properly.

In 1991, there wasn't much of a team defensive structure or system like there is nowadays. You just had to keep your man scoreless and hope that your teammates did the same, and the result would take care of itself. I think there's more protection for defenders now, with 13 of 14 lads back inside their own half most of the time. There's definitely less space for forwards.

We definitely hung on at the end of that final and won it by just a point, although it really could have gone either way again. Derek was on form, and he scored eight points for us. Anthony Finnerty scored a goal for them in the second-half to give set up a nervy finish. I think he may have nudged Des Newton in the back just before it too, so it would have been hard on us if Mayo went on to win after that.

They didn't though and the crowd flooding onto the pitch at the end was surreal. That was something a young lad like me would never have encountered before. Sure, you'd have it after a county final win, but nowhere near the scale of what we experienced that day at the Hyde. I think the official attendance was something like 24,000 but there must have been far more than that by the end! The buzz in town afterwards too… it was brilliant craic. That feeling lasted for about two or three days in Roscommon town afterwards. Everyone was on a high.

When the celebrations died down, we started our preparations for the All-Ireland semi-final. Meath were our opponents, and they had a very good team then. They had played Dublin four times in the Leinster Championship that year, so I think the semi-final was their ninth game in total that summer. We had played just three, including the replayed final against Mayo.

One funny memory I have is of our preparation in the Hyde Centre. To get used to the idea of running out in front of 60,000 or so people at Croke Park, the backroom would play crowd noises over the speakers. For some people it was a bit of a laugh, while others thought it was genius. Marty McDermott must have been ahead of his time because I think Mikel Arteta did something similar with his Arsenal players before a big match at Anfield recently!

I'm sure if word got out back then about that part of our preparation, the reaction would have been along the lines of *F****** eejits, what are they at?* But just look at the levels of preparation nowadays, and even the kind of backroom set-ups most counties have. Players these days have tags and sensors on their backs during games to track their mileage. We would have been afraid the manager was tracking us to the pub!

That Meath game was definitely one that got away from us. We were a few points up at one stage near the end but ended up losing by a point. It was devastating. We had a great chance to win that match and reach an All-Ireland final. We went from such a high after the Mayo game to such a low in the space of just two weeks. It was hard to take.

My abiding memories are of the good times playing for Roscommon, though. As I've said before, I was very lucky to play with some of the best footballers this county has ever seen. Brilliant players like John Newton, Des Newton, and Tony McManus. Pat Doorey was the full-back and he was probably coming near the end of his time with the county. But by Jesus, he'd go through a wall. He was one *hardy* buck! You'd be a bit fearless knowing if anybody messed with you, Pat would be in there straight away.

Against Meath, it was Pat, Des and me up against Colm O'Rourke, Brian Stafford and Bernard Flynn, who won an All Star each that year. It was always going to be a tough ask, but I think we acquitted ourselves well and we were just unfortunate we couldn't manage to see out the game.

In terms of honours, 1991 was probably the highlight of my time with Roscommon. I played for 10 years or so, retiring in 2000 and only got the one Connacht title out of it. If someone had told me that summer that there wouldn't be another Connacht medal, I would have found it very difficult to believe them. I played in a couple more finals with Roscommon and we had some brilliant championship wins, but that was as good as it got.

In terms of silverware, I was lucky to be playing club football with Clann na nGael in those years. We won seven county titles and two Connacht titles, and should have won an All-Ireland club title too.

As regards individual honours, I've always felt you're only as good as the team that's around you. Whether it's a Player of the Year award, an All Star, or even a Connacht or All-Ireland medal, you won't ever win it on your own. You need a good team of guys around you and that includes the subs and the whole wider panel too. I think I played decent enough football that year... I must have done to win an All Star! I marked Bernard Flynn in the semi-final and kept him to a point. He was one of the top guys at that stage so that probably clinched the award for me. Though, as my old friend Finbar Egan pointed out to me afterwards... 'How much did ye lose by?'

There would be no fear of something like an All Star going to your head... certainly not in Clann country anyway!

DEREK DUGGAN

MEATH 0-15 ★ ROSCOMMON 1-11
All-Ireland SFC Semi-Final
Croke Park, Dublin
AUGUST 18, 1991

★ **ROSCOMMON:** G Sheeran; D Newton, P Doorey, E Gavin; J Connaughton, P Hickey, M Reilly; S Killoran, J Newton; V Glennon, T McManus, T Grehan; E McManus Junior (0-3), P Earley, **D Duggan (1-8)**. **Subs:** M Donlon for Glennon, D O'Connor for Reilly.

★ **MEATH:** M McQuillan; B Reilly, M Lyons, T Ferguson; K Foley, L Harnan, M O'Connell (0-1); L Hayes, PJ Gillic (0-1); D Beggy (0-1), T Dowd (0-2), C Coyle; C O'Rourke, B Stafford (0-9, 5 frees), B Flynn (0-1). **Sub:** G McEntee for Ferguson.

❝

I WAS JUST out of the minors before the Connacht Championship in 1991, so of course I was very enthusiastic and had my heart set on making it onto the first team. There were a few challenge games just before the championship started and I remember doing quite well in those. This was a whole new experience for me, but I was excited and looking forward to our first match against Leitrim that summer.

My call up to the senior panel came after the 1990 county championship. I had been part of the Castlerea St Kevin's team that made the final that year against a formidable Clann na nGael. Both teams were at two different ends of the scale really, but we had one thing in common... the number seven. We had around seven minors playing for us that day, while Clann were going for their SEVENTH county title in-a-row! Needless to say, Clann won and won well that

THE ACTION

★★★★★

THE ROYALS HAD just come through an extremely difficult Leinster Championship campaign which included four epic games against their fierce rivals Dublin. Sean Boylan's men were forced to dig deeper than deep to keep their summer alive.

Marty McDermott's charges took an early lead through the superb Derek Duggan, before Brian Stafford, who like Duggan, was to have a memorable game, kicked Meath's opening point but despite some bad wides, Roscommon still held a commanding 0-5 to 0-1 lead after just 15 minutes.

Then, just when it looked like Meath had battled their way back into contention with points from Tommy Dowd, Martin O'Connell and David Beggy, up stepped Duggan to blast Roscommon into a 1-7 to 0-7 half-time lead. The talented young forward sold Terry Ferguson a wonderful dummy solo before rifling the ball on the half-volley past McQuillan.

After 15 minutes of the second half, they had stretched their lead to 1-10 to 0-8. Their good attacking play was built on the foundations of hard defensive work. Des Newton and Enon Gavin had marked Bernard Flynn and Colm O'Rourke out of the game essentially, but the Roscommon defenders just couldn't cope with Brian Stafford and Tommy Dowd.

Stafford had the game of his life, while Dowd was proving to be a handful even for the impressive Rossie defence. Three points in-a-row from Stafford meant that Roscommon's lead was cut to the bare minimum with just three minutes remaining. The Connacht champions had just run out of legs in the end and the Meath sharpshooter sent over the equaliser and then from the kickout pointed to give Meath the lead.

★★★★★

day, but I put in a decent performance. On the back of that, Marty McDermott called me up into the Roscommon senior setup.

Most young players would have been fairly apprehensive going into such an experienced Roscommon dressing-room, but I had been playing senior football for a few years at this stage and so knew most of the big characters. That didn't mean it wasn't a bit daunting at first, however! But I have to say my overriding memory is that it was a mature Roscommon team and every one of them made me feel welcome. I received massive encouragement… it's great for a young fella to go into an environment like that because you can just concentrate on playing your own game.

I was delighted to get a start against Leitrim in the Connacht semi-final. Marty and his management team showed a lot of faith in me, and, like my teammates, they offered plenty of encouragement too. Of course, being young and inexperienced, I had no idea how my first taste of championship would go…

I remember being quite nervous in the first-half and I did struggle to get into the flow of the game. All you can do in that situation is stick at it, really, and get a few simple touches. Luckily, I scored a good point from out near the sideline just before half-time. That score was crucial for me because I felt I hadn't done a whole lot in that first-half and was probably at risk of being hooked off!

I settled into it after that and even flourished a bit in the second-half with another two points. We won by four points in the end against what was a very good Leitrim team at the time.

After a performance like that, there is always an extra boost in training, especially when you know you're facing Mayo in the final. I was only 19 but some of the other lads had won a Connacht medal the year before. They were looking forward to another final and in their minds, they were the favourites. There was certainly no fear in the camp, in fact they were looking forward to getting a crack at Mayo.

I was living in Castlerea near the Mayo border at that time. My father is a Mayo man and I had relatives who were Mayo, so the atmosphere in the lead up to the game was brilliant around the home house. I was only dying to go training and I just couldn't wait for the game itself. Back then, you'd have over 30,000 crammed into MacHale Park and something similar at Dr Hyde Park. Both grounds were teeming for the games. There was a fantastic atmosphere before and after both games. It felt like a real championship summer.

The drawn game in Castlebar is the game I'm usually asked most about. We were a point down with time almost up when we were awarded a free not too far inside Mayo's half. I won't lie and say the free was a blur because I do remember it quite well! People might look back and add an extra bit of analysis to it, and maybe describe it as 'a pressure kick' but when you're out there lining it up you don't really feel that pressure... you don't have time to! You might get nervous before a game but as soon as that ball is thrown in your focus is entirely on each play.

Perhaps the real reason I didn't feel any pressure on that kick was that no one told me it was the last kick of the game! I was fairly oblivious to that at the time, and I remember I made a few dummy runs to receive a short kick from my Castlerea clubmate, Mattie Reilly. We soon gave up on that idea and he called me over to take it. I'd played with Mattie for several years and I guess he knew what I was capable of from a dead ball. Being young, I didn't have any fear so over I trotted to place the ball.

I vividly remember looking up at the posts way down the other end of the field and seeing all the players jostling each other around the square. I also remember the supporters massed behind the goal. On the one hand, you had Mayo supporters offering up prayers that I'd miss, and on the other hand, you had Roscommon people hoping for another day out! I was just thinking, *Right, I have to hit this on the button.* My confidence was high and all the frees I took were from the ground anyway, so this situation wasn't anything new... in my head at least! I focused on my technique and making sure I made good contact and, thankfully, the ball flew over the bar.

We were relieved to get another crack at it in the replay, particularly at home in Dr Hyde Park. We managed to just about get the job done the second day by a single point to make it back-to-back Connacht titles. I ended up with a total of 14 points over the two games, including 0-8 in the replay, so I was more than happy with my own contribution.

There was so much experience in that team. I was getting huge encouragement from Tony McManus, Paul Earley, John Newton and those older guys all the time. That meant you could play without fear really.

I've seen situations where talented young players were thrown into teams that didn't have that level of experience. The pressure becomes too much for them and they're just not able to perform. That certainly wasn't my experience with Roscommon. I was able to flourish from that very early stage. Youth is brilliant that way too; you don't see any pitfalls. All you see are positives and silver linings, and all the good things that could happen.

Next up for us that summer was another formidable outfit in the shape of Leinster champions, Meath. Despite their reputation and the fact that they were clearly battle hardened following an epic duel with Dublin over four games, confidence in our camp was high going into that semi-final.

Don't get me wrong, we had an awful lot of respect for Meath. We knew we were putting ourselves up against the best, but we relished that. Most sportspeople want to test themselves against the best and see how good they are, and we were certainly no different.

We really believed we were good enough to win, and a lot of the aspects of the game went well for us. We had a good start and went 0-5 to 0-1 up, and then typical Meath, they clawed their way back... again!

Just before half-time, I got an opportunity. Tony McManus kicked a ball into me, and I found myself in loads of space in front of The Hill. I saw the Meath goal in front of me and thought, *I'm going to have a crack here*. I could see Terry Ferguson out of the corner of my eye as he was advancing towards me. I knew what I was going to do with it... it was as if it happened in slow motion.

Dummy solo.

Ferguson out of the game.

Then... BANG.

I would have practiced a lot of drop-kicks in training, so it was pure instinct in that moment.

It was a great feeling when the ball hit the back of the net. It felt like the whole of Croke Park shook! The Hill was buzzing at the time, and I could *feel* the ground shake beneath me.

The hardest part was the celebration... I didn't know what to do with myself! Initially I ran in the direction of the Rossies on Hill 16, turned back, and then did a couple of fist pumps before getting ready again for the Meath kickout. That roar was something I had never experienced before; it was just a brilliant feeling.

But... in trademark Meath style, they came back at us again. My goal was nearly on the stroke of half-time, but they went straight down the other end and scored what was probably the most important point of the game. PJ Gillic put one over from about 50 metres out and instead of going in four points up, we went in with a lead of three. That was a massive point for Meath.

We were still in a great position at half-time and it was all positive in the dressing-room. We even found ourselves *five* points up at one stage early in the second-half. It was 1-10 to 0-8 about halfway through that second-half. We seemed to be in a great position…

But from there until the final whistle, I don't know what happened. Did we go too negative to protect our lead? It was partly that, but it was also down to just how good that Meath team was. They were chipping away at our lead all the time. We only managed one point after that.

Meath never panicked. But why would they? All the experience they had, as well as those four brilliant matches against Dublin earlier in the summer… they must have felt bullet-proof in Croke Park by then!

Every time we looked back on that game in the years that followed it was seen as one that we let slip away. We just didn't score enough when we were on top and paid the price for it in the end.

On a personal level, I was happy to a degree with my performance against Meath in that All-Ireland semi-final. I scored 1-8 on the day but looking back, there's always a tinge of regret that you couldn't get on a bit more ball and get a few more scores to make the difference. In the end, we still lost the game, which was a huge disappointment. You always think if you'd just had a couple more chances it might have been a different result.

Meath lost the final to Down and I have to say I don't believe there would have been very much between ourselves and the Ulster champions. I think Down caught Meath on the back foot early on, because a few things went against The Royals in the lead up to that final. They had a couple of injuries and I think Colm O'Rourke was sick that week too. I always felt that if Meath hadn't had such a bad start, they would have won that game comfortably. So, it was nearly more of a regret that we didn't see it through against Meath because we probably had the measure of Down, or at the very least, we would have had a great chance of beating them.

Losing that match to Meath is probably the biggest regret of my time with Roscommon.

Paul Earley had a few great chances early on. He had the beating of Mick Lyons. On another day he might have had two or three points scored but between being unlucky and then Mickey McQuillan pulling off a great save, it just wasn't meant to be.

We could have been a lot further ahead in that game. I'm not saying we could have had the 11-point lead Down had at one stage in the final, but maybe a four- or five-point advantage at half-time. I think if we had kept them out before the break and managed to add to our lead early in the second-half, then we would have held out for a place in the final.

So, it's definitely a *big* regret…

When the final whistle blew, I was hugely disappointed, *Jesus, the summer's over. That's it.* But looking around the pitch, I could see even more hurt in some of the older guys. They realised how big an opportunity this was, having been there for so many years. Of course, 19-year-old me thought we'd be there again the following year… and the year after and so on. Obviously, it doesn't work out that way. Fellas retire, the team changes and there might be a few injuries. Suddenly, it's a long time before you're back in Croke Park again. And it was a long time, another 10 years, before we won another Connacht title after that.

I didn't think of that at the time or right afterwards. The dressing-room is quiet after such a big loss, and you don't tend to dwell on your own performance. It's a funny feeling when you play well and lose, because it is a team game at the end of the day, and the final result is really all that matters.

In the weeks after that you might feel a sense of satisfaction in playing well but it's very hard to revel in it. We've seen it in the last few years when a member of a losing team wins the Man of the Match award and they're being interviewed afterwards. It's a hollow prize in many respects because you'd sacrifice not playing well to win the trophy or even to reach an All-Ireland final.

Since I retired from football, I've often been asked how I felt when I scored a particular point or goal. I can tell you that as soon as that ball is thrown in you don't get much time to feel anything really. You might score a great goal or an important point, but as soon as you start clapping yourself on the back that's when you're in trouble. You're standing there feeling proud of yourself, and meanwhile your marker might go up the other end of the field and score one himself. Sometimes you're at your most vulnerable when you do get a good score... and Meath's point before half-time in 1991 is evidence of that.

It's the same for bad misses too... there's no point in dwelling on them because you might miss the next opportunity that comes along. The key to playing well and a lot of success on the field is simply staying in the moment. That's where training and practice and all the hard work beforehand is so important. It all comes to fruition in a match, and you go out and do things on instinct. At the top level there is just no time to think or feel. The best players make the right decisions at the right time.

There's no question that Meath game was one that got away, and I've always said that. It was one that 'got away' in the sense that if we had won it, I think we would have been in a brilliant position to win an All-Ireland. A first All-Ireland in almost 50 years for Roscommon.

Unfortunately, since that year, Roscommon teams haven't really threatened an All-Ireland title even though we've played some brilliant stuff in Connacht and won a number of provincial championships.

In 1991, there was no question we were good enough to win an All-Ireland final. Five points up halfway through the second-half against Meath... the regret was not closing it out. You could go through the game and pick out things that we could have prevented or could have done better, but even the best teams need luck.

Meath probably needed it that summer against Dublin, but unfortunately it ran out for them in the final against Down. Our luck ran out in that semi-final. If we had a bit more of a rub of the green, Roscommon could have won a third All-Ireland title that year. We were that close...

25

OF THE
GREATEST
IN ACTION

★★★★★

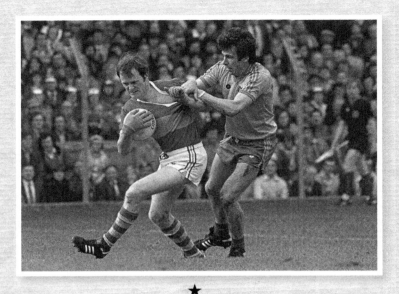

★

*Ger O'Driscoll finds his path blocked by Pat Lindsay,
as Roscommon came so close to beating Kerry in
the 1980 All-Ireland final*

★

*Mickey Menton offering his
support from the sideline*

Former Roscommon players in attendance at the inaugural GPA Former Players Network event in 2013. Front row (from left): Tony Kenny, Vinnie Glennon, Christy Grogan, Mark O'Gara and Tom Heneghan. Back row (from left): Martin McDermott, Harry Keegan, Seamus Hayden, Gerry Fitzmaurice, Tom Hunt, Gay Sheeran and John O'Callaghan.

 Des Newton learned from some of the best, like All-Ireland Under-21 winning manager, Tom Heneghan, and also took his own turn as Roscommon team boss

★ *Gerry Fitzmaurice adding his expertise to the Roscommon line in 2007, with manager John Maughan*

★ Tony McManus (back row, third from left) and Harry Keegan (front row, third from left) and the 'Football Stars of the 80s' were presented at Croke Park in 2013

★
*DANNY MURRAY in typical
swashbuckling style*

★
*Derek Thompson
in Connacht
Championship action
against Galway in 2001*

★

Seamus Killoran in action against Colm McManamon of Mayo during the Connacht Championship final in MacHale Park in 1991

★

John Newton rises highest against Brian Moylan of Galway in the Connacht final in the Hyde in 1990

Enon Gavin breaks past James Horan of Mayo in the 1999 Connacht Championship

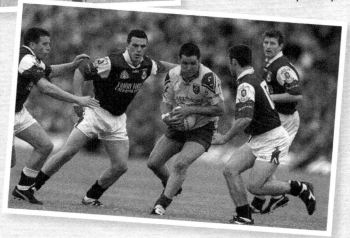

 Derek Duggan in typical pose, weighing up another spectacular score

 Francie Grehan in his favourite place in the whole world, surrounded by Galwaymen in the 2001 championship

★

Fergal O'Donnell presents the Nestor Cup to Roscommon's loyal fans in 2001

★

Gerry Lohan celebrates putting one away against London in 2000

★

The amazing Shane Curran leads the Roscommon team into championship action in 2004

 The industrious
Cathal Cregg wins
another ball against
Sligo in the 2010
Connacht final
victory

★ Senan Kilbride
celebrates with
his brother, Ian
after Connacht
Championship
glory for St
Brigid's in 2011

★

The lethal Donie Shine Jnr shoots another one over, this time in the 2014 championship

★

Conor Devaney surges up the field against Galway in the Connacht final in 2017 in Salthill

Frankie Dolan relishes the last gasp victory over Ballymun Kickhams when St Brigid's were the first team to bring All-Ireland senior club honours back to Roscommon

Seán McDermott in action against Donegal in the All-Ireland Championship in 2018

★

Enda Smith is still dreaming the dream, and proving a powerhouse as Roscommon chase after the Sam Maguire Cup

FRANCIE GREHAN

ROSCOMMON 2-12 ★ GALWAY 0-14
Connacht SFC Semi-Final
Tuam Stadium
JUNE 3, 2001

★ **ROSCOMMON:** D Thompson; D Gavin (0-1), J Whyte, M Raftery; P Noone (0-1), **F Grehan**, C McDonald; S O'Neill (0-2), F O'Donnell; C Connelly, J Hanley, A Nolan; N Dineen (1-3), G Lohan (0-1), F Dolan (1-2). **Subs:** G Cox for Nolan, S Lohan (0-2) for Dolan, R Owens for Raftery.

★ **GALWAY:** P Lally; R Fahey, G Fahey, T Mannion; D Meehan, J Divilly, S De Paor; S Ó Domhnaill, J Bergin (0-1); T Joyce (0-1), J Fallon, M Donnellan (0-1); A Kerins (0-1), P Joyce (0-6), K Comer (0-1). **Subs:** J Donnellan (0-3) for T Joyce, K Walsh for Comer, R Silke for Divilly, L Colleran for Ó Domhnaill.

I HAD BEEN playing at centre-forward just before Christmas 2001, but I felt like I was going nowhere with it to be honest. It had even got to the stage where I was seriously considering packing county football in altogether. By God, I'm glad I didn't! Fergal O'Donnell had been made captain that year and word must have got out that I was thinking about walking away, because he phoned me one evening and pleaded with me to stick around. That was all the convincing I needed, and I made my mind up there and then to put everything into it that year.

I must have been taking it seriously because I decided I wasn't going to have a drop of drink over the Christmas break. Not one drop! I felt if I was to make an impact on the team then I'd have to take my fitness up a level, and so that's what I did. Christmas Eve pints and a drink with the dinner were replaced with extra workouts.

THE ACTION

★★★★★

ROSCOMMON WEATHERED AN early Galway storm before getting on top in the midfield sector thanks in no small part to the efforts of 19-year-old Seamus O'Neill. When Nigel Dineen grabbed a goal after just 12 minutes, Roscommon supporters could even dare to dream, perhaps for the first time that day.

Galway, however, led by the inspirational Padraig Joyce, had managed to develop a 0-8 to 1-4 lead heading into injury-time at the end of the first-half.

Normal service looked set to resume before another Rossie young gun came to the fore. Frankie Dolan ripped up the script as he smacked home Roscommon's second goal of the afternoon right on the stroke of half-time..

With their tails up, Roscommon continued to dominate on the resumption and while Galway briefly levelled matters by the 50th minute, Roscommon, with the inspirational O'Neill dominating at midfield, finished the stronger of the two. Two points from substitute Stephen Lohan gave them much-needed breathing space in the closing stages as they sealed their place in a Connacht final at Dr Hyde Park.

There were a number of standout performers for the Rossies that day, not least the aforementioned O'Neill at midfield. However, it would be fair to say this Roscommon success was built on solid defensive foundations and they didn't come much more solid than Francie Grehan at centre-back that day.

★★★★★

I remember an incident when Gay Sheeran was manager in the years before 2001. A few of us had been out on the beer one weekend and one of his 'spotters' reported us. Gay wasn't too happy and pulled a few of the lads aside after training to let them know in no uncertain terms how he felt. The trick was, if you went on the beer after a match, then just make sure you're one of the best trainers the following Tuesday evening. That was something I was very good at. I'd make sure I was up at the front for all the running… so Gay couldn't pin a night out on me!

'There was another lad involved,' he told the 'guilty' ones that night, 'But we just can't prove it because of the way he's training at the moment!'

Practicing temporary abstinence must have paid off in 2001 because our manager, John Tobin arrived up at the house one evening before a league game with some interesting news.

'You'll be playing at centre-back this weekend,' he told me. That was the night my career with Roscommon was really transformed. That decision helped to turn it around for me.

I felt that the change in position was brought about by my own change in attitude. I showed how seriously I was taking it that winter and some of the sacrifices I made were beginning to pay off on the pitch.

We had a good league campaign that year and played Mayo in the semi-final a couple of weeks before the start of the championship. Mayo beat us by two or three points in Markiewicz Park, but it didn't feel like they were a much better team or anything like that.

I suppose we were happy enough going into our opening championship game against New York at Dr Hyde Park. This would be the last time New York would travel to Ireland for a game for a long time. We were absolutely shocking that day. We won by 10 points in the end, but I remember the scoreline flattered us a bit. Never mind, we were through to a semi-final against Galway in Tuam.

There are no two ways about it: any game against Galway – championship or not – always takes on more significance for me because of where I come from. Ballyforan is located smack bang on the border separating the two counties, and so the build-up to big matches is always that bit more intense than it is in other parts of Roscommon. If you're not hearing about it from Galway supporters, then you're being told how important it is to win by the Roscommon fans. The local bragging rights are nearly more important than the Nestor Cup!

One thing that sticks in my mind is that following the league campaign that year, a local paper ran an article rating each player's overall performance. One journalist was a bit critical of my own performances and basically said that while I had had a good league campaign, I'd be roasted in the championship. That was something that really got my back up going into the games against New York and then Galway.

The training under John Tobin was really tough, but you felt like you were really getting somewhere with it. It was a good set-up in fairness, but I suppose I would say that when my father, Frank was involved! Toby had Des Ryan doing the strength and conditioning, and he was top class. We also had Jimmy Finnegan as selector, the Lord have mercy on him. Jimmy had been involved with successful Roscommon minor teams the years before, so knew the scene.

My own preparation was… intense. I was going out to my sister, Mary's house the month before the Galway game. I had that critical newspaper column, hinting that I was too slow for championship football, stuck on the kitchen wall. I'd look at it most days before I went training. It was a like a scene out of the Rocky movies!

Every night after training, my sister would help me through some extra exercises. We'd do a stretching programme and then she'd have me doing runs using a 'bungee cord' in the garden. This went on for the whole month. Looking back, I'd say John Tobin was delighted that column was published!

Look, I was always the kind of fella who, if you praised me, I'd go to a certain level, but if you doubted me or questioned my ability, I'd take it to a whole new extreme. I never wanted the arm around the shoulder, but you never needed to give me a kick in the arse either. Now, if you said to me, 'You can't do this, Francie' or 'You're not good enough'… well, that's when my famed pig-headedness would kick it and I'd move Heaven and Earth to prove you wrong.

In fairness to Toby, he was great with me. He'd call out to the house regularly in the lead up to the Galway game with videos of Ja Fallon, who I'd be marking in Tuam. It was a good psychological ploy by Toby because by the time the week of the game came around, I was so fired up I just wanted to be out on the pitch.

I remember on the day of the semi-final we togged out in St Pat's in Tuam. We had these Errea tracksuits which were all the rage back then. Really shiny yokes… horrific. I still have nightmares about them to this day! I wouldn't mind but it was the only bit of gear we got. Toby had this idea that we'd get ready and then walk up to the ground as part of the warm-up. We walked alright, but not one of us was brave enough to put on that tracksuit! It was a good thing too because as we were making our way down towards the ground, I spotted six of my own teammates from St Aidan's walking just ahead of me… each of them wearing Galway jerseys. That was like a red… or maroon flag to a bull!

There was a good Roscommon contingent there that day but nothing like what you'd expect for a Connacht final say. It could have been a case that our supporters weren't expecting a lot from us following our league defeat to Mayo, and our unconvincing win over New York. Galway were one of the best teams in the country at that stage too and had only been beaten after a replay in the All-Ireland final the year before.

We were out on the pitch before Galway, and I remember chatting to Fergie O'Donnell and Clifford McDonald in the middle of the field shortly before throw-in. I was feeling good, and I was really fired up for the match… and for Ja Fallon.

Maybe I was a little too fired up…

Less than a minute after the throw-in the referee was calling me over. Ja received the ball with his back to goal and before he could get a turn on me, I pole-axed him. It was a yellow card and it meant I would be walking a bit of a tightrope for the rest of the match. That's a long 70-plus minutes when marking someone like Ja!

I don't think the caution changed my mentality. I still had a job to do, and I think you need to play on the edge sometimes, especially if you want to be able to live with some of the best attackers. If anything, that incident settled me a bit because I knew I'd have to focus on my football from then on.

We started the match reasonably well apart from that incident. We had Seamus O'Neill playing at midfield. He was only 19 and Toby had been careful to mind him a bit during the league that year. It was paying off now.

There was a bit of a *eureka* moment in the first few minutes when I knew the extra training in my sister's garden was paying off. The ball broke and I was in a foot-race with Ja towards the end line. He had a bit of a head start as we made a burst for it. I ended up nicking in ahead of him and my confidence went through the roof after that.

Toby's style of play was centred around first-time ball into the full-forward line. We had a very strong inside line with Nigel Dineen, Gerry Lohan and Frankie Dolan. It was something very few teams could live with. This way of playing really suited me because it meant I got on the ball a good bit more from centre-back. Kicking the ball was one of my strengths, and there were plenty of opportunities to do that in Tuam.

The Galway team from 1998 to 2001 had some serious footballers to be fair and Michael Donnellan was one of the best around. Paul Noone had to be at his very best for us, and he was. He had a serious performance that day. So did Cliffy McDonald on Joe Bergin. Cliffy was probably giving away around five or six inches in height but still managed to keep him relatively quiet.

People talk about the final win over Mayo that year at the Hyde, but I think that game against Galway was our best performance overall. There were great displays all over the field that day, but the one they were all talking about was Seamie O'Neill. He caught everything.

It was only much later, during the Covid lockdown, that my father and I sat down to watch that match back. One player who really stood out was Conor Connelly, Lord rest him. He was phenomenal that day, head and shoulders above everyone else on the pitch.

Toby's tactics worked perfectly in that match, and Nigel and Frankie scored two early goals to take the sting out of Galway. We got better and better then as the game went on. It was the kind of performance you didn't want to end.

It's not very often Roscommon would be on top of Galway in their own backyard. This was a Galway team that had been All-Ireland champions just three years before. Ja Fallon was also Player of the Year in 1998 too. They were unfortunate not to have won in 2000. But we used all of that as motivation. We loved being the underdogs and putting it up to them.

That's not to say it was all plain sailing for us. There was one moment when we feared the momentum might turn. John Donnellan came onto the field and won a free about 50 yards from goal out near the sideline. He kicked over a monster score and there was a deafening roar from the Galway supporters. All of a sudden, he was the big man in Tuam and Galway looked up for the fight. That was until Ronan Owens, or 'Shovels' as we used to call him, was brought on to mark him. John scored three points in total that afternoon, but from what I remember, Shovels kept him to a point from there until the final whistle, and that was a consolation free.

I always felt we were in control, especially in the second-half. But there was another incident that probably should have been a turning point for Galway. Frankie Dolan was heading through on goal when he injured his shoulder. He collapsed to his knees in agony and coughed up possession. Galway came right down the other end of the field, but thankfully Ciaran Comer missed a glorious goal chance. It later turned out that Frankie had dislocated his shoulder and would be a major doubt for the Connacht final.

When the final whistle went, a few of the journalists wanted to chat with me. I declined them all. I felt as though I had proved a point on the field that day. It was never in my mind to come out and do an interview, like Kieran Donaghy and say, 'Well lads, what ye think of THAT?'

Anyway, I was delighted I decided to give the media a miss that day in Tuam because the great Jimmy Murray arrived in our dressing-room to sing The West's Awake. He gave us a rendition of that song a few times down the years, but he seemed to really enjoy singing it in Tuam.

To top off a great day in Galway, we took our time going home and visited a few of the local pubs along the way… just to let them know who we were, like!

We were given a warm welcome in Moylough because a buddy of mine owned the pub. But the reception in Newbridge was a bit frostier, especially seeing as the barman served four of the lads… but refused to serve me. I realised there and then, that I didn't like Galway but maybe they didn't like me either!

Going to the pub works both ways when you're a Roscommon footballer, or probably any county footballer for that matter. We'd usually go back to The Royal Hotel in Roscommon for a bit of grub and a couple of pints after matches. You'd be mingling with the supporters too. Well, after losing to Leitrim in 2000 I was absolutely rail-roasted! And guess what, the very same fellas were coming up and patting me on the back in 2001. I don't forget these things!

Thankfully, the disappointment of seeing my own St Aidan's teammates supporting Galway earlier in the day was made a little easier later that evening. I had put a friendly £20 wager on with one of the Galway lads back home in Ballyforan, and so I made it my business to sit up on the bridge and wait for him to come present me with my winnings! It's a very tribal thing in Ballyforan… though that's probably the wrong word to use. Both sets of supporters are very much diehards and there's always that bit of tension when the counties meet. No one wants to lose those matches because life could quickly become unbearable in the village!

The win over Galway set us up nicely for a home Connacht final against Mayo. Toby must have been happy with the way our walk through Tuam worked out in the semi-final because he made us walk from The Abbey Hotel to the Hyde for the final too. Thank God it was far too warm for those Errea tracksuits!

That was another tough match, but we came through it thanks to a goal in injury-time from Gerry Lohan. It was another brilliant day and night in Roscommon, and the celebrations afterwards were something else. The only problem was that we then had a six-week break before our next match, an All-Ireland quarter-final against… Galway! We had a long lay-off, but Galway had played three matches and so were maybe that little bit sharper. Unfortunately, beating All-Ireland contenders twice in the same year was always going to be a big ask.

While we didn't go on to win an All-Ireland ourselves, there were so many great characters in that Roscommon team. We were a very close-knit group too. After the game you'd stay in town with the lads and go for a few pints. The quiet lads were always the biggest troublemakers. Great men like Denis Gavin and Paul Noone, who never made the papers! It was always great craic.

I remember afterwards being chosen to play for Ireland in the Compromise Rules and a journalist asked, 'Is this the proudest moment of your career?' I said no. 'The 2001 Connacht final then?' No, it was the semi-final against Galway. It was just a great feeling and it's not often we got the better of them. They were a serious team with some wonderful footballers. And to beat them in Tuam, as well… it was just a brilliant day, especially for a man from Ballyforan!

There was one other man who was delighted we'd won too… my nephew, Jack Heneghan. Jack had arrived into the world in May of that year, just in time for championship football. Jack's father and Fergal O'Donnell would also have been close. It was decided the best thing to do with young Jack would be to wait until after the Connacht final and Christen him in the Nestor Cup… and that's exactly what we did!

99

GERRY LOHAN
(& FERGAL O'DONNELL)

ROSCOMMON 2-10 ★ MAYO 1-12
Connacht Senior Football Championship Final
Dr Hyde Park
JULY 1, 2001

★ **ROSCOMMON:** D Thompson; D Gavin, J Whyte, M Ryan; C McDonald, F Grehan, P Noone; **F O'Donnell**, S O'Neill (0-2); C Connelly (0-1), J Hanley (0-1), S Lohan (0-1); N Dineen, **G Lohan (2-2)**, F Dolan (0-3). **Subs:** G Cox for Dineen, D Connellan for S Lohan, J Dunning for Hanley, A Nolan for Connellan.

★ **MAYO:** P Burke; G Ruane, K Cahill, R Connelly; A Roche, J Nallen, N Connelly; P Fallon, C McManamon (0-1); J Gill, K McDonald (0-4), T Mortimer (0-1); M McNicholas (0-1), M Sheridan (0-4), S Carolan (0-1). **Subs:** M Moyle for Gill, D Nestor (1-0) for Carolan, D Brady for McNicholas.

❝

WHEN MY BROTHERS and I were growing up, our dad, Eddie Snr, the Lord have Mercy on him, would bring us to all the Roscommon games, even though he himself was a Galway man. Our mam, Mary, came from Mayo but she was always adamant that she'd be too nervous to go to games with the rest of us.

There's no doubt you make great friends playing Gaelic football at any level, but especially so when representing your county. I was lucky I got to play with some exceptional fellas and even togged out with my two brothers, Stephen and Eddie in championship and Division One matches.

Maybe there were some mixed feelings for our parents with the Galway and Mayo connections. I'm not sure they weren't a bit torn when we came up against their own counties. Ah, but they always backed us to be fair… at least to our faces anyway!

THE ACTION

★★★★★

BLISTERING SUNSHINE, RED cards, late drama and a manic pitch invasion... the Connacht final of 2001 had it all! But it was the Rossies who were left the happier of the two teams by the half-time whistle as they led 0-7 to 0-5.

The second half was even more eventful. All in all, there were three goals, 10 points, two red cards, and one massive Primrose and Blue pitch invasion. Mayo were at their most dangerous in the third quarter and had levelled matters at 0-10 each with 12 minutes left to play.

Then, a major turning point, Ray Connellan was sent to the line after referee Seamus McCormack consulted with his umpires. It seems Connellan had got involved in an off-the-ball incident with Roscommon forward Frankie Dolan. The numbers on both sides were now even following Clifford McDonald's earlier dismissal for Roscommon.

If the first 60 minutes were entertaining, the final 15 or so were Oscar worthy in terms of the drama on show. It started seven minutes from full-time with Gerry Lohan making no mistake in finishing low to Peter Burke's net.

Points from Kieran McDonald and Maurice Sheridan were followed by an injury-time goal for David Nestor to give Mayo a two-point lead deep into time added on. Suddenly, it looked like curtains for Roscommon as the supporters in green and red prepared to celebrate a famous victory behind enemy lines.

★★★★★

I was first called into the Roscommon senior set-up at the age of 18 in 1998 under Gay Sheeran. Gay was in charge for the following two years as well, until John Tobin took over in late 2001. To me, there wasn't much difference between the two men. They were both good managers. The only noticeable change was having a new voice in the dressing-room and, of course, new selectors and a new trainer. We had more or less the same group of players that I had made my debut with in 1998, plus five or six new fellas who had broken into the panel that year.

Our championship campaign that year started against New York in what would be their final match outside the United States. This was just a few months before the 9/11 terrorist attacks too which would have a big impact on teams travelling across the Atlantic to play them.

Playing for Roscommon, you'd always be expected to get the job done against New York, especially at home, and we beat them fairly handy at the Hyde that year by 3-13 to 1-9. I scored five points that day, and Frankie Dolan and Nigel Dineen got our goals. We were off and running, but we knew there would be much tougher games to play that summer.

The semi-final put us against Galway in Tuam. That was a very good Galway team and that year they went on to win the All-Ireland, gaining some revenge on us in the All-Ireland quarter-finals.

We played brilliantly in Tuam in the semi-final in June, with Dineen and Dolan in great form once again. It was a very tough game, but the reward was a Connacht final against Mayo at Dr Hyde Park and when we saw the crowds in town, we knew we had to make home advantage count.

On the morning of the game, we met in The Abbey Hotel and John Tobin decided that because it was such a nice day, we would walk down to the Hyde with the Roscommon supporters. That is something I will never forget!

Down the 'County Home Road' we went, and in through the back entrance of Hyde Park. It was just brilliant. The whole day was brilliant… well apart from maybe the 72nd to the 75th minutes of the match. But we came out on the right end of it at the full-time whistle.

On the walk down, I remember we were in groups of twos and threes, and we were mingling with the supporters. I'm sure they were a bit surprised to see us, in fairness. They were full of chat about the game, of course, and everyone was wishing us the best of luck. They were pleading with us not to lose… 'NOT AT

HOME TO MAYO!'

The excitement that day was something else. I don't think any of the modern football managers would allow players to walk to the ground these days. To be fair, it might have been a different story if we lost to Mayo in that final. I think the lads nowadays get the Club Rossie bus down to the Hyde and teams even arrive for matches in Croke Park with a Garda escort. Thinking about some of the lads we had on our team in those days, I don't think a Garda escort was needed anyway!

I think the walk worked for us… it helped us to relax a bit before the game. You got to soak up the positive atmosphere too. Saying that, home advantage was great, but there was also added pressure on us. We had to make sure our biggest rivals didn't turn us over and win a Connacht title in our own backyard. That would have been very hard to take for our supporters, and it had happened before.

The game itself was fairly end-to-end. The pace was unreal in that heat. I remember Conor Connelly, God rest him, scoring an excellent point early on. Sadly, Conor passed away just a few years ago but he's certainly someone that those of us who were lucky enough to have played with him will always remember, both on and off the field.

I was marking Kevin Cahill that day and I don't think I did too bad! I scored two goals and two points, only scoring my first goal seven minutes from full-time. Mayo have always had good defenders and you would never get anything too soft against them anyway, no matter who was picking you up. As we know, even today, they always have a very strong defence. I've always thought goalkeeper to midfield were their strongest sectors.

We had a good team at that time too, and it was really back and forth for the whole game. It could have gone either way. I remember we were a few points up at one stage and they came back into it. Then David Nestor scored a goal in injury-time to put them two up. We were so caught up in the game that we didn't realise how late it was. Afterwards, our goalkeeper Derek Thompson said he thought there was about 10 minutes left on the clock even at that stage.

I think the official attendance was around 30,000 that day but I'm nearly sure two or three thousand had already left after that late Mayo goal. A few people said it to me afterwards that they were in at Casey's heading for the pub when I scored my second goal. I won't mention any names!

There was no such thing as 'possession football' back then. You were told to let the ball in early to the forwards. It's a good job 'playing down the clock' wasn't really the done-thing either, because Mayo ended up giving up the ball away a bit cheaply a few minutes later. In fairness to them, they were always trying to do the right thing and attack. But they kicked it out over the sideline with time almost up, which gave us a chance to launch one last attack. The only problem, from our point of view, was that the ball was deep in our own half and the seconds were ticking away. There was still a lot of work to do to get it within range of the Mayo goal.

I still remember the build-up so clearly. The sideline was put into the Mayo half of the field and Johnny Dunning fetched it from the air between two defenders. Johnny gave it to Denis Gavin who moved it on to me…

I feinted to my right…

Skipped back onto my left…

Peter Burke and his two defenders bought it.

And I blasted the ball low into his net with my left foot.

Francie Grehan had run past me as I received the ball. Maybe the easy thing to do would have been to give it to him. Frankie Dolan was also inside waiting for a hand-pass, but that would have been a bit more difficult to execute. It would have been an easy goal for Frankie if I'd managed to find him alright… but Francie might have blasted the ball wide!

My belief when in on goal is that you should always try and roll the ball in, if possible. Just place it. There's no need to be blasting the net out of it. Also, aim to pass it into the net low because most goalkeepers will find it harder to get down there. Don't leave it at a nice height for them, whatever you do.

Scoring a goal for Roscommon is special of course, but you only really think about how it feels when you look back. At the time, you don't pass too much heed on it because it's all about the team. It's great for the supporters but you're really doing it for the 35 or 36 guys on the panel in the course of the year. We were the lucky ones to be in the starting 15 and that's the reality of it. You have to do those other guys justice on the day.

The final whistle was such a relief that day, and the celebrations that followed in Roscommon and further afield are probably legendary at this stage. There was still an All-Ireland quarter-final to come but I think we went off on the beer for about a week after that! There were bucks hurting themselves doing handstands on nights out and, suddenly, Galway in Castlebar was looming. I don't think we were fully right for that game, if I'm honest. Galway were a savage team back then too and were competing for All-Irelands every year. Beating them twice in the same championship was always going to be a tall order.

On a more positive note, Roscommon town the night of that Connacht final win over Mayo was absolutely outrageous. Just unreal. We had food in The Abbey Hotel and then we headed to 'Down the Hatch', which is run by former Roscommon player, Seamus Hayden and Larry Brennan. We visited The Red Parrot, John O's… I won't name them all, but we were in A LOT of pubs and the town was just chaotic.

The next day we went back to 'The Hatch' early and spent another day on the beer. I think we even found the energy for a repeat visit to the Parrot too. It was great craic, it really was. Sure, if you can't celebrate the good times…

You see, the county hadn't won a Connacht title in 10 years, since 1991, and to do it in front of thousands of our own people made it extra special. You have to remember too that there was a month between the two games, which was really not good for us. It benefitted Galway more because they had a couple of qualifying games in between and could build momentum and maintain a bit of focus. I think losing in the Connacht Championship gave them added motivation too. Sometimes going through the 'back door' works better for teams in the long run. I think we've seen that with Mayo in recent years too.

There's no doubt Galway were waiting in the long grass for us ahead of that quarter-final in Castlebar, and they deservedly won that day before going on to lift the Sam Maguire that September. While it didn't work out for us with Roscommon, at least there was one happy man in the Lohan house that year!

★ ★ ★ ★ ★

FERGAL O'DONNELL

66

I SUPPOSE YOU can't really talk about the Connacht final of 2001 without mentioning our disappointing Connacht Championship campaign the year before. That year we lost to Leitrim in the semi-finals in a game we should really have won at Dr Hyde Park. It was a game we were well ahead in, but we missed numerous goal chances and Leitrim hung on in there and knocked us out.

That was Gay Sheeran's last game as manager. It had started so well for him in 1998 but what a sad way for it to end. We had been unlucky to lose to Galway in his first year and they went on to win the All-Ireland. In 1999, we took a bit of a beating in Castlebar. But we were going well in 2000, until that game against Leitrim.

Following the Leitrim defeat there was a lot of talk about whether Gay would stay on. I think people would have been happy if he had. It was the players, not the management team that hadn't performed. It went back to 1998 and the fact that we hadn't built on the progress made that year. We might have made the mistake of thinking, *Jesus, we were within a kick of a ball of beating Galway...* and got complacent. There were also injuries and lads retiring too, so all in all, about six or seven changes in those three years from 1998 to '01.

We did get ourselves back on track in 2000 in the National League and we were well set going into that Leitrim game. We should have killed them off in the first-half, but we didn't. As a group, we definitely could have done better that day.

The big thing about 2001, apart from the change in management from Gay Sheeran to John Tobin, was the change in the championship format to include the qualifiers. It wasn't something that we gave too much thought to at the time, but it would prove to be hugely important in the years that followed, setting the scene for some great days out for Roscommon. I would have known John Tobin because he had managed Galway, and when I was younger, he was also in charge of Tuam CBS. He was well known as a coach, although I think he was a surprise selection at the time. I'm not sure many would have thought of John as Gay's replacement.

One of the clever things John did was he brought Frank Grehan in with him. Frank had had good success with the under-21s previously. He also brought in Jimmy Finnegan, who had worked with the minors and won a provincial title. Gary Wynne was involved too, so he surrounded himself with a very good backroom team. Another big coup was the arrival of Des Ryan as strength and conditioning coach. Des would go on to work with Arsenal Football Club later in his career.

The gym became a big part of our training. Paul Gilligan was involved, and our strength work had become more structured. Before that, we were doing our own thing really with a few of us doing gym sessions in Boyle and Carrick. Believe it or not, gyms weren't as plentiful as they are now, so you were sometimes forced to travel a bit to get access to weights.

Our training base was in Ballyforan, and I just remember those sessions being absolutely savage. Nowadays, there's a lot of talk about 'training load' and the importance of rest days. There's no way the current lads would be training as hard or as often as we were that year. There was a lot of speed and agility training, and the tackle bags became an important piece of equipment too. I remember running into the likes of Francie Grehan, Nigel Dineen, Peter Mahon... those guys had massive strength. Six players would hold tackle bags and the other guys would run at them and hit them. I don't know which was worse, holding a bag or hitting them!

We also had three vs three mini games focused on tackling. Frank Grehan refereed them and by God, he let an awful lot go!

Another important aspect of our training were our A and B games. Later on in the year, we even travelled to Tuam to play an A v B game the week before our Connacht semi-final against Galway. I just remember it being very, very tetchy. Frank must have been reffing that one too! He was a tough taskmaster. I think one of the lads ended up kicking the ball out of Tuam Stadium in frustration with some of the decisions!

The Foot and Mouth Disease was a major worry early in 2001. It led to the postponement of a couple of league games. We were a bit stop-start and lost our first two games, and had only one win prior to Christmas 2000, but our form improved dramatically after that. We beat Dublin and Kerry, and that was a big thing for me because I was coming up against the likes of Darragh Ó Sé and Ciaran Whelan in midfield. There were quality teams around at that stage and we finished second in the Division One table just behind Galway. Mayo won it out that year after finishing ahead of Sligo in Division 1B. Not unlike 2023, Connacht football was in a good place in the league that year.

We got as far as the league semi-final against Mayo at Markiewicz Park. We fell away badly at the end of the game, but it gave us great hope going forward. Mayo went on to beat Galway in the final, but we knew we weren't far off that level.

John Tobin did a bit of video work with us around that time, and he was very much into moving the ball forward quickly. If you look at the quality we had in that inside line – Nigel Dineen, Gerry Lohan and Frankie Dolan – then getting quick ball into them made perfect sense. At that stage, Francie Grehan had moved from No 11 to No 6 too. It was a clever move because Francie was one of the best passers around at that time. I remember we analysed that Mayo league semi-final with Toby, and he highlighted the forwards' work rate and maybe the midfield being a bit slack. He told us we were grand going forwards but defensively there were areas we needed to improve on.

Our opening championship game was against New York and there was all sorts going on. There were stories going around that the New York players were partying most of that week... it didn't seem that way at Hyde Park! Shane Curran was a bit unfortunate to be sent off in that match too. It was a difficult game to play in because we were expected to win, but we didn't play that well and only managed to pull away in the second-half.

That game created a few opportunities for lads, I think. Seamus O'Neill wouldn't have played against New York; he only arrived into the team for the semi-final against Galway in Tuam. There were a lot of good players in the squad but during the New York game it just didn't happen for some fellas, and Toby showed he wasn't afraid to make changes. Seamie's inclusion in the following games was one of the biggest decisions and it led to him having an unbelievable debut season.

We noticed major improvements on the training ground that year. The sessions had been improving since Christmas and the quality was seriously good going into the championship. There were real leaders in the group too, the likes of Clifford McDonald, who had been centre-back and captain in previous years, Conor Connelly, Stephen Lohan… I was lucky enough to captain the team, but there were leaders all over the pitch.

I was appointed captain under Toby. He just rang and told me he wanted me to be captain for the year. I was married in September 2000, so I'd returned to training a bit late at the start of the season. I was surprised that he picked me, but I was obviously delighted too.

I can't fully remember the conversation about it, but he did mention my performances the previous year. I had played wing-forward, but he saw me as playing more centrally. He also felt that we weren't too far off and believed there was a lot of quality in the team.

Toby had great knowledge of the school system too. Gerry Lohan and Paul Noone were two lads who came from a very good CBS team in 1998. Gerry was the main player there and Toby had been a corner-forward himself, so he had a real eye for quality attackers. He very much had the type of team he wanted when it came to the full-forward line. Nigel Dineen was the strong man who could win ball and take his man on and score, while the two lads playing off him, Frankie and Gerry, were two very skilful players.

I had a good working relationship with Toby throughout the year in our manager and captain roles. We spoke about where we needed to improve, and he'd listen to my opinion. But he very much made up his own mind with help from an impressive backroom team.

While it was a very close-knit group, one or two players did leave during the year because they weren't getting game-time. That was difficult because I felt if they'd hung around, they would have been given opportunities. But that happens with every squad and it's understandable that lads don't want to be giving up their time if they're not playing.

It was an honour to play for Roscommon and it's only when you finish playing and you're managing teams that you fully realise what a privilege it is. Suddenly, you're cutting lads from panels, and you see how disappointed they are not to represent their county. Anyone who reaches the level of getting into a county panel has definitely got something about them in terms of commitment and ability. That's for sure.

Being captain, you're a link between the players and management. The biggest thing sometimes as captain is not the younger players, it's those lads who aren't playing regularly. That's something I would have found difficult because you're dealing with guys you may have soldiered with a couple of years before and now they're not getting as much game-time. It's the likes of them you have to look out for because they're still putting in the same amount of effort as the lads who are playing. You're trying to encourage them and keep them going because a squad is built on competition in training and the quality in the wider group.

The big thing I remember about the build-up to that year's Connacht final was the colour around the place. We had beaten Galway in the semi-final, a team that had been in the All-Ireland final the year before. We were then playing Mayo who were the reigning league champions. It's very similar to Roscommon this year (2023) with the three Connacht teams taking the top three spots in the National League. The difference was that Mayo and Galway didn't go on and win Sam this year whereas when we were playing, Galway did.

I was very nervous in the car on the way up to The Abbey ahead of that final. I think my wife, Marie drove me up from Boyle, and I just remember the nerves. We saw the flags and bunting in Elphin and all the good luck messages in Tulsk… and for the lads in Kilbride. There was Primrose and Blue all the way up.

We met in The Abbey Hotel and there was a great buzz among the players. John had us walk to the pitch in Tuam and he did the same that day in Roscommon. That was very different because normally we'd travel in cars. Mick Mullen was the kitman and he took our bags and off we went out the County Home Road.

Toby's view was that you got a feel for the match day atmosphere on the way into the ground. I don't know whether I'd recommend that now as a manager myself! To be fair, I don't know whether it was a good thing or a bad thing, but it was definitely unusual! The strangest thing about it was not having my kit bag on my back because normally when you were going training or walking into the Hyde, you'd be carrying your bag.

When we ran out onto the pitch that day, the noise was just deafening. That's something I remember about the replay in 1998 too. It was a hot day and the colour around the place was unbelievable. The number of jerseys and flags was a sight to behold…

The pace of the game was electric early on. I remember making a pass to either

Francie or Cliffy, and Trevor Mortimer came in and hit me a savage shoulder just as I released the ball. It shook every bone in my body. I had a pain in the back of my head for a few minutes after. I picked myself up thinking, JESUS, am I alright? I think I was more surprised that it was Mortimer. If it was Colm McManamon or Pat Fallon, then you'd maybe understand. The only other player who'd ever hit me as hard before was Darragh Ó Sé. He hit me a shoulder and put me to ground. This time I managed to stay on my feet and keep running… but I was shaken to my core.

It was tit-for-tat between the sides after the opening minutes. There were a lot of mistakes, and I lost the ball myself at one stage and Francie Grehan got on to me about it. Then shortly after, I got on the ball and did something positive, and there he was shouting encouragement. That's something that's always stuck with me. Yes, get on to fellas when they make a mistake but give them that encouragement too.

I don't remember Gerry's first goal, but I do remember his second. When they scored their goal, I made sure to get on to the lads the way Francie had encouraged me. It was a case of 'Heads up lads, we go again'.

They had another chance to attack near the end, but I think it was David Nestor who flicked the ball out over the sideline. There was another attack too when McManamon was soloing in, and myself and Cliffy got across to block. There were two or three moments like that towards the end that could have put them two or three scores up… and out of sight. There was a stage when we were trailing at the very end and part of me thought, *Jesus, this just isn't going to happen for us.*

Then Johnny Dunning made that outrageous catch between two Mayo players. I couldn't even remember Johnny coming on, and I'm not sure he ever made a catch like that before or since! He was a great forward though and he served Roscommon so well when we needed him most. That was another game-changing moment, and it allowed us in for one last opportunity.

Johnny reacted quickly when he came down with the ball and passed it to Dinny Gavin. You wouldn't expect Dinny to be up there! The ball was given in to Gerry, and Gerry as cool as a breeze, slotted it into the net. It was a brilliant finish because he still had plenty of work to do. I just remember the place going mental… and the excitement on the pitch. Peter Burke kicked the ball out and the full-time whistle went.

There was a feeling of disbelief that we'd won it. I just remember the crowd on the pitch after that and RTÉ pulling me in to do an interview. Two guys from Boyle came running by roaring, 'Ten f"""""years!' It had been a long wait since 1991 for our fantastic supporters. It was just brilliant to see how happy they were on the pitch at the full-time whistle.

We brought the Nestor Cup back to The Abbey Hotel. There were crowds of people looking to get their picture taken. There was this woman, who lived in Tubbercurry but was always a great Roscommon supporter. She was there with her daughter who had special needs. Having my picture taken with them and seeing how much that day meant to them is still something that sticks with me.

There was a real party atmosphere. I think we took the cup out to bingo at the Hyde and then out to the Sacred Heart Hospital. The county board chairman, Stephen Bannon was with me, and I remember him dropping me out to my mam and dad's house afterwards. It was a special feeling landing in home. Mam and dad were delighted. The buzz that night in town was something else too.

There's nothing between winning and losing those matches. I was just glad we came out on the right side of the result because it was such a thrill to be captain that day. In terms of performance, I felt the team had played better in the semi-final in Tuam, but then we were coming up against a quality and experienced Mayo side.

Gerry stole the show with two goals, and I think he was 'Sports Star of the Week' in the *Irish Independent* too. You appreciated winning more when you've lost a few. Playing with Roscommon Gaels, we had lost a couple of Connacht finals in the years before. With Roscommon, we'd lost to Galway in 1998. The Gaels' drawn game with Crossmolina and that Galway game were two I thought we should have won. But then sometimes you just don't get the rub of the green. We got the rub against Mayo with our goals because they probably had enough chances to put that game beyond us.

That Roscommon side had great team spirit and some quality players. You don't realise how good some of them are at the time and maybe you don't fully appreciate how special days like that are either. We played some very high profile matches in those years between Division One league games, Connacht finals and the All-Ireland quarter-final that year against Galway. There were performances of real quality from many of those players. In Tobin's two years, fellas reached another level. But the highlight was that Connacht final at the Hyde. Nothing could compare to that moment when Gerry's shot hit the net… and then the crowds on the pitch after. Contrast that to the feeling after 1998… 2001 WAS special. After losing to Leitrim the year before, I was beginning to think it would never happen.

To carry the Nestor Cup and be lifted shoulder high by people you don't know and who may even have been cheering against you in club football just weeks before… that's just magic. This is it. This is what we dream for. In that moment, all the sacrifices are worth it. And there is a lot of sacrifice involved in playing for your county. I was 29 at that stage and I'd had to miss stag parties, weddings, and other nights out, or even time with family because we'd be in training or preparing for matches. The biggest regret is that we didn't have more success or build on that win.

Winning at the Hyde and of course Roscommon Gaels being a huge part of me, meant I got to see all the people who were working on the committee and who had supported me from under-12s right the way up. People like Harry Hoare, Jimmy Mannion, and all those people who introduced me to football. Also meeting teachers and the trainers you might have had. It was also special for that panel to have Jimmy Finnegan and Frank Grehan involved because they'd trained Roscommon teams to minor and under-21 titles. That's something else Toby did brilliantly. He called on the experience that was at hand in Roscommon. It wasn't the 'Toby Show'… it was a Roscommon one.

Throughout my career with Roscommon, I was very lucky to experience winning as a player, a captain and as a manager. Winning as a manager is different because you're more hoping for the lads to perform and get over the line. Players probably put too much pressure on themselves to perform and that's the one thing I realised when I stopped playing, that I was worrying about too many things I shouldn't have.

Roscommon don't win too many Connacht titles, when you think about it. Even winning in 2017 and '19, we probably would have expected to have won another one since. It was the same for Roscommon Gaels. We won a club title in 1994 and felt we could go on and win more. All of a sudden, 20 years have come and gone…

The most important thing though was representing Roscommon and our supporters. We've a great 'away' support, particularly if you look at National League matches in different parts of the country. It's impressive because Roscommon wouldn't have a large population, but our support is always massive. When you're wearing that jersey and you're facing the tricolour for *Amhrán na bhFiann* and looking out at the town… and over towards the Sacred Heart Church, well, for those couple of minutes at least, you're unbeatable.

SHANE CURRAN

ROSCOMMON 1-18 ★ KILDARE 0-19 (AET)
All-Ireland Qualifier
O'Moore Park, Portlaoise
JULY 26, 2003

★ **ROSCOMMON: S Curran**; R Cox, D Casey, J Whyte; M Beirne, F Grehan, P Noone; S O'Neill, S Lohan; G Cox, G Lohan (0-1), D Connellan; J Dunning (0-1), K Mannion (0-3), F Dolan (0-13). **Subs:** J Tiernan (1-0) for G Lohan (42), E Towey for Noone (49), B Higgins for Connellan (60), N Dineen for Dunning, M Ryan for Whyte, J Rogers for G Cox, G Ahearne for Casey.

★ **KILDARE:** E Murphy; B Lacey, D Lyons, M Dunne; M Wright, G Ryan, A McLoughlin; R Sweeney, K Brennan; P Murray (0-6), J Doyle (0-2), P Hurley (0-2); P Brennan (0-6), K Donnelly, T Fennin (0-2). **Subs:** D Hendy for Lyons, E Callaghan for Dunne, D McCormack for Murray, T Rossiter (0-1) for Donnelly, E McCormack for Doyle, D Lyons for Brennan, N Browne for Hurley.

66

THE SUMMER OF 2003 was such an exciting adventure through the qualifiers and one I think our supporters really enjoyed. There was a last-ditch goal against Leitrim and then the 'Frankie Dolan Show' against both Offaly and Kildare. He hit 0-12 against the Faithful County and then somehow went one better with 0-13 against the Lilywhites. It was magical stuff.

There was the Tommy Carr story too. He took us from the depths of despair, following the 'Naked Pool' incident in Derry in 2002, and turned us into a well organised and competitive unit. A lot of that was down to the players too and also the fact that Tommy started picking the county's best players. For many years, perhaps that wasn't always the case, whether one likes to admit that or not!

I found Tommy brilliant. He made me captain, of course, but I had a great relationship with him anyway. I captained the county for two years and that's

THE ACTION

★★★★★

WHILE ROSCOMMON WERE considered by some inside and outside the county as the swashbuckling misfits of Gaelic football, Kildare were a gritty and determined outfit, who had previously ruled the roost in Leinster.

While a well-taken John Tiernan goal would prove crucial for the Rossies, the major headline of the afternoon centred around St Brigid's sharpshooter, Frankie Dolan, who scored an outrageous total of 13 points, including six from play, and a couple of screamers right from the very top drawer. Put simply, Dolan was unplayable once again, and he forced the game into extra-time with a massive score right at the death.

Dolan continued where he left off in extra-time, but just when it looked like Roscommon were home and hosed, Kildare fought back with a couple of points from Pauric Brennan. The already depleted Lilywhites were hit with a further blow, however, when Tadhg Fennin was sent off for a second bookable offence after clashing with goalkeeper, Shane Curran.

Frankie then sealed a memorable day for both himself, and for Roscommon football, as he added another three points to seal progression to the All-Ireland quarter-finals. The scenes at the end were reminiscent of a Connacht final or All-Ireland win as the Roscommon supporters invaded the pitch to celebrate with their heroes. It was a day when the Roscommon sporting public gladly welcomed its county senior football team back in from the cold following that harsh and sometimes bitter year of 2002.

★★★★★

something I'll always be very proud of. Tommy had a good support staff too; Jimmy Deane was with him, and so was Gary Wynne. Sean Finnegan, who went on to work with Kevin McStay at Mayo, was also part of the team. Everything was very well organised.

We'd been beaten by Galway in the Connacht Championship and so it was decided we'd take off to La Manga in Spain to do a hard week of warm weather training. To be fair to Tommy Carr, it was all very professional. It was all part of a fresh start after 2002.

A fresh start was all well and good, but that didn't mean the messing and antics had to stop completely, of course! One incident that stands out occurred just prior to the throw-in of that championship game against Galway in Salthill, an episode I blame Adrian Tully for!

Uhlsport were my sponsors at the time so there was no problem in getting a pair of gloves. Adrian and myself concocted a plan at the time to smear Vaseline on one pair of gloves and when the march around the pitch was over, I'd shake hands with Galway goalkeeper, Alan Keane. I remember running over to Alan and giving him a lovely firm handshake using both hands and wishing him to best of brotherhood from a fellow member of The Goalkeepers' Union! The plan was to target Alan early on, before he realised what had happened. In the meantime, Adrian had gone down to our goal and left a fresh, clean pair of gloves for me.

I think there was a bit of consternation down at the other end when Alan realised what had happened. He was stomping around his goalmouth and calling for another pair of gloves, but we didn't get an opportunity to take advantage.

It was one of those things. You're looking for any sort of edge in a big match like that and seeing if you can get into your opponent's head. It probably wrecked his head for a couple of minutes, but it certainly didn't have any effect on the scoreboard, and we would eventually lose the match by four points.

Word must have got around after that prank in Salthill because for the two years I was captain after that, no one would shake my hand. They wouldn't even trust a fist-pump! I remember we played Dublin the following year and Stephen Cluxton saying, 'No way, I'm not shaking that!'

When it came to the captaincy, however, I took my role very seriously and would sometimes employ unusual tactics in order to gee the lads up before big games or at half-time if I thought we needed a boost. It was during the interval of that Galway game that I decided to spill blood for the cause… or at least tried to!

I went to our team doctor, Martin Daly a couple of weeks before with an unusual request. I told him I was feeling a bit stressed out or run down, and I needed to have blood taken, and then stored in a bag. I don't think he had any clue what I had in mind. If he had, I've no doubt he would have told me where to go! I remember bringing the bag home and the look on my wife, Sharon's face when I arrived in.

'What do you want that for?'

'Don't worry about it, just stick it in the fridge'.

I took it out the night before the Galway game and threw it into my bag, along with the rest of my gear. I had it all planned out. I knew what I wanted to say to the lads if things weren't going our way at the break, and how the bag of blood would come into play.

We came into the dressing-room at half-time and things certainly weren't going our way. I'd already got a bit of a bollocking from the Galway lads because I don't think their manager, John O'Mahony was too happy about the vaseline incident earlier.

I felt we needed a bit a *Braveheart* speech or something to get us back into the match. I took out the bag of blood and in a fit of temper, tried to burst it off the floor. I was hoping the blood would splash over all the lads and then I'd deliver the killer line, something about needing to… *spill Roscommon blood for the cause.*

Looking back, it was a good job the bag didn't burst, because I don't think we would have been going back out for the second-half if it had. It just bounced off the concrete and lay there in solidarity with the floor!

We ran back out for the second-half and ended up losing anyway, so the bag of blood obviously didn't have the required effect.

We went on a bit of journey in the qualifiers that year. We had the late Jimmy 'Nail' O'Connor goal against Leitrim, and we had a narrow win over Cork at the Hyde, another game I fondly remember. Our campaign rolled on to Offaly and then Kildare in the qualifiers, so we played five championship games before bowing out to Kerry in the All-Ireland quarter-finals that year.

Looking back on that campaign, we were probably one of the few Roscommon teams to beat teams from three different provinces in championship football in the same year. Obviously, we didn't get to the All-Ireland final, but it was like a mini-All-Ireland run for us.

That meeting against Kildare was for a place in the last eight against Kerry, which would be played at Croke Park. As Roscommon players, we wouldn't have played a lot of championship football at headquarters, and our supporters were definitely enjoying their regular days out at that stage!

That round four qualifier was a huge game for us, and the stakes were very high. There was a feeling that we didn't really perform against Galway in Salthill that year so to get to a quarter-final against Kerry would have been a pretty good return for us.

The players were also looking for redemption that year after the county board disbanded the team at the back end the previous year. La Manga, where we had our training camp, was famous as not only a training base for the English soccer team, but also for its nightlife too. But I think we'd had enough of the parties after 2002!

It's easy to look back now and say the gap between our Spanish training camp and the championship could have perhaps been a bit wider, but I do think it stood to us in our long run of matches later that summer.

My role as goalkeeper was different to a lot of lads in other counties. I look at the likes of Ethan Rafferty with Armagh now and how he plays as an extra outfield player at times. That was something I was doing back in 2003. Tommy saw it as 'risk-reward' and I would've been briefed before games on where the opposition might target me. We did a lot of tactical work and worked a lot on the kickouts too, because we had really good fielders around the midfield sector.

Fergal O'Donnell had gone by that stage, but the likes of Seamus O'Neill and Stephen Lohan were still there, while Karol Mannion from St Brigid's had also come into the fray.

Prior to that Kildare game, we had a team meeting at a hotel in Portlaoise. Tommy had everything set out for us. We went through the Kildare team and through our own roles.

'Keep it tight lads, but play on the front foot with confidence,' Tommy told us. Once Frankie got going that day, the crowd just lit up. You could feel the energy and enthusiasm flowing off the terraces. It felt like the whole county was behind us and everyone had come along on this roll we were on.

There was bedlam in Portlaoise that day at the full-time whistle. I do think we were the better team by a considerable stretch, even though it ended up going right down to the wire. It went into extra-time, and I got involved in a bit of controversy with Tadhg Fennin and got him sent off.

I suppose the Statute of Limitations is up for that incident so I can talk about it freely now! It was hard on Tadhg and especially considering it was a second yellow card offence, with the first card coming in normal time.

I don't feel like I had anything to do with the decision, really. I was hit and went down and then got up… and the umpire pulled him on it. There weren't really any theatrics or anything. It was just because of the speed I was travelling at – sure, I was like a Ferrari in those days! Just like Cristiano Ronaldo or Mohamed Salah… any little trip or contact, it would make me lose balance! To be honest, I couldn't believe he was sent off. Tadhg didn't say much to me after.

In fairness to the Kildare players, they were magnanimous at the full-time whistle. I was fairly friendly with Johnny Doyle, and he accepted we were the better team on the day. They were in transition with a new management team. They were probably changing a bit from the team that had been relatively successful in the years previous, winning Leinster titles in 1998 and 2000, and reaching an All-Ireland final in '98.

For Roscommon, it was a great day. I remember walking back out of the ground with the supporters. I was in a hurry because my cousin was getting married, and I wanted to make the 'afters' of the wedding. Sure, we didn't get back until around eleven or twelve that night because there was such jocularity around the place. We eventually arrived back and had a few pints in the hotel with our families and supporters before setting our sights on Croke Park, and the mighty Kerry the following week.

Looking back on the summer of 2003, four championship wins remains quite significant. I don't think it's happened to too many teams since… even those that have won Connacht Championships.

There was a great vibe. The county board were also right behind us, and great credit must go to the chairperson, Stephen Banahan. It had been a difficult time for Roscommon football, but he was terrific throughout that period. I always look back on my time fondly as Stephen was very good to the players.

That beautiful summer of 2003 was the peak of my time with Roscommon. I don't like looking back and saying it was all so much better in our day; we had a great time playing though. We enjoyed pulling on that jersey on days like that in Portlaoise and while we probably should have won more Connacht titles or gone further in the All-Ireland series, I feel like we left people with good memories of that era. That's really what it's all about, at the end of the day.

I think it's the same for the lads playing today. Yes, they're under more pressure in terms of expectations, but that pressure is a privilege. You have to embrace it when you're playing the game because that's why you are a footballer.

Embrace that pressure and privilege that comes with wearing the Roscommon jersey. I only wish I could've worn it for 35 or 40 years. I often remember Tommy Carr saying he'd love to play one more game. It's only now that I can't, that those words really resonate with me…

I was fortunate, however, that I was able to play for another 10 years at club level and I can look back on a great career, and say I really enjoyed every minute of it.

99

DONIE SHINE JNR

ROSCOMMON 1-10 ★ KERRY 0-9
All-Ireland MFC Final Replay
Cusack Park, Ennis
SEPTEMBER 23, 2006

★ **ROSCOMMON:** M Miley; P Domican, P Gleeson, S Ormbsy; N Carty, D Flynn, C Garvey; D Keenan, **D Shine (0-6)**; F Cregg (0-1), D O'Gara (1-1), K Waldron; P Garvey, J McKeague, C Devaney (0-1). **Subs:** C McHugh for McKeague, A O'Hara (0-1) for Garvey.

★ **KERRY:** T Mac an tSaoir; B Russell, M Moloney, D Ó Sé; S Enright, A Greaney, B Costello; T Walsh (0-2), D Moran; P Curtin, G O'Driscoll, J Buckley; G Sayers (0-1), P Curran (0-4), E Kennedy (0-2) **Subs:** D O'Shea for Buckley, S Browne for Costello, J Dolan for Curtin.

WITH ALL DUE RESPECT to other management teams and coaches I have had, I would say that the Roscommon minor team of 2006 was the first real professional set-up a lot of us were part of. We were so well prepared, trained really hard, and on top of all that, had a really strong group of players that year.

The round robin section of the Connacht Championship went very much according to plan, and we beat both Sligo and Leitrim by three points in two low-scoring games. I know it's cliché, but we really were only taking it one game at a time. We beat Galway in the Connacht semi-final, and then the summer just seemed to stretch out before us. Suddenly, we were in a position none of us ever thought we'd be.

We'd had a pretty forgettable league campaign that year, losing all games along with some challenge matches. That will tell you where we were going into that

THE ACTION

★★★★★

A YOUNG AND talented Roscommon team had won the hearts of the county's football supporters and their dogged determination was evident the first day out against Kerry. That game had ended in a draw at Croke Park, meaning both sides would have to do it all again in Ennis.

This was to be one of the most memorable Roscommon performances of all, at any grade. Each member of the team played their part in stifling a talented Kerry outfit. Mark Miley's kickouts were laser-guided, reducing the effectiveness of the likes of Tommy Walsh. There were star performers in every line, with David Keenan and Donie Shine on top at midfield, and David O'Gara grabbing a crucial goal early in the second-half.

With the game level at 1-6 to 0-9 heading into the last 10 minutes, it was the Connacht underdogs who surged for home. Shine hit the final three scores of the match, including two from play. Kerry didn't register a single score in the last 18 minutes as Roscommon smothered them in the Ennis sunshine.

As the final whistle blew and it was confirmed that Roscommon had won their first All-Ireland title at this grade in 55 years, the Primrose and Blue-clad supporters flooded onto the pitch to embrace their newest heroes. The celebrations would continue all the way back to Roscommon and in the weeks that followed too.

★★★★★

championship in terms of results. Despite that, we always believed in what we were doing and the direction in which the team was going. There were no doubts around our training and preparation, and both the management and players had a feeling that it would eventually click into place for us.

Each win in the championship really filled us with huge amounts of belief and confidence, and it got to the stage where we were almost afraid to lose. That fear then became the ultimate motivation, as we won the Connacht title against Mayo in Castlebar and went on to the All-Ireland series.

We met Tipperary in our quarter-final in Tullamore. They were a good team, but they'd lost the Munster final by eight points to Kerry, who hadn't won an All-Ireland minor title in over 10 years. The Ulster teams were quite dominant around that time and Down were the defending champions, having beaten Mayo in the final the year before. Our confidence was high after beating Mayo in our provincial final and we swept past Tipp fairly convincingly to set up a semi-final against Leinster champions, Meath.

Meath had come through quite a competitive Leinster Championship that year but those of us who went to school in Athlone had come up against most of their players in colleges football. We knew that they were a really good team, but we had a massive work ethic at that point, and we were willing to do whatever it took to reach the All-Ireland final.

It helped that we were so well prepared by Fergal O'Donnell and his backroom team too. They put on some really good training camps in The Curragh around that time. The great Dermot Earley would also call in to visit us from time to time and just his presence was enough to give us all a big lift.

The Meath game was a much bigger test than our encounter with Tipperary, but we managed to come through it with four points to spare in the end, winning 1-10 to 0-9 at Croke Park. Roscommon would be competing for an All-Ireland minor title for the first time since 1951... 55 years is a long time to wait for anything!

The one thing I have a very clear recollection of from that summer, and our road to Croker and ultimately to Ennis, is just how hard the training was! If you missed even a couple of sessions, you were simply left behind. It was all very sharp in terms of going from drill to drill. No one was left standing around and everyone took it very seriously. You'd soon had one of the coaching staff on your case if they didn't feel you were putting in the right amount of effort. There was a huge amount of tackling and defensive work… yeah, those sessions were *tough*!

Another thing that stands out was the level of opposition preparation. That was something else most of us wouldn't have experienced before. From video work to team meetings and analysis, you felt like you had every base covered. There were also the one-to-one meetings with the management team where we identified areas to improve on. It was all just taken to a completely different level. It was all very new back then and we were lucky to be exposed to it. There's no doubt in my mind that our preparation was the difference in allowing us to have a proper crack at an All-Ireland title that year.

We did a lot of video work in the build-up to the All-Ireland final. We must have watched Kerry's semi-final win over Donegal a dozen times! The one thing that was very clear from watching them was that they were on a different level to any other team we had played so far. It was very hard to miss the likes of Tommy Walsh at midfield or David Moran at wing-forward. It seemed as though they were already playing at senior level at that time.

Even before that first match at Croke Park, I remember walking out and looking down the other end of the pitch and thinking, *JESUS! Look at the size of them!* Tommy Walsh was definitely built like a senior player and that kind of thing can be intimidating when you're 16 or 17 and still developing. Was it 'advantage Kerry' before a ball was thrown in? Well, you try to not let it get to you, but some of our players were definitely talking about it.

As it happened, we were lucky to cling on early in that first game. We were 0-8 to 0-3 down at one stage and the game was slipping away from us. If the next score had gone against us, we could have been finished. Luckily, we warmed to it and managed to stage a late rally in the first-half to reduce the arrears to two points at half-time. That felt significant at the time, and it would prove crucial by the end of 60 minutes.

While we were 'lucky' in the sense that Kerry weren't further ahead, our preparation had been spot on once again. Fergal and his backroom team had identified the 10 minutes before and 10 minutes after half-time as key phases in the game. We wanted to attack those 20 minutes with everything we had. We had won games during those phases and while we had to settle for a draw that day in

Croke Park, it gave us great confidence that we could go one better in the replay.

Fighting back the way we did against Kerry galvanised us, I felt. Just having the experience of playing Kerry and learning a bit more about them was huge. We then had another week of preparation in order to find a way to counteract them.

One thing that we needed to improve on was our kickout strategy, and I know our goalkeeper was up at his local pitch in Knockcroghery each morning with a bag of footballs. There was no real hard work done that week. It was all about finding subtle little ways to tip the balance in the replay.

The big thing for me in any game was getting off to a solid start, and just doing the simple things right. When you have responsibility for frees, you don't want to be putting yourself under extra pressure by missing a few early on. It's important to get that first score for confidence sake.

In the first game, I managed to kick a couple of scores before being shipped out to midfield to deal with Tommy Walsh. I struggled for good chunks of the game as he won a lot of kickouts over me. But I stuck at it, and it helped that I had a lot of positive people around me. The likes of David Keenan and David Flynn had huge work ethic and a really positive mindset. They were constantly in your ear. Those two were so important for the team. Their attitude was fantastic. Overall, it's probably fair to say that the first game looked to be getting away from us and there was certainly huge relief at the full-time whistle that we hadn't lost it.

There were moments, particularly in the first-half, where I thought, *Yeah, this isn't going to be our day.* We managed to turn it around in that second-half and even went three points up at one stage. So, yeah, we *could* have won it… but we had to be happy with the draw in the end. The replay was fixed for Cusack Park in Ennis. Little did we know what we were facing into!

We felt really good going down to Clare because we knew were capable of competing with Kerry after earning a draw at Croke Park. We were in a really good place and then word starts filtering through about the size of the Roscommon crowd making their way down. It gives you a lift knowing your people will be there to cheer you on.

We had stayed in Ennis the night before to avoid any delays due to the traffic, and it was a good job we did! It seemed like everyone in Roscommon had made their way towards Cusack Park that day. Later, we would hear stories of supporters giving up on trying to reach the ground and instead watching the match in various pubs along the route.

I remember my own preparation was quite poor on the day, funnily enough. I ripped my boots during the first game in Croke Park, so I went out and bought a new pair. I still kept the old, ripped pair in my kitbag… just in case! Of course, there wasn't enough time to break the new boots in and they just didn't feel right. I switched pairs a number of times during the warm-up. It wasn't ideal. Small details like that can scupper you. It's just a case of keeping your head down once the game starts and trying to blank out those distractions.

Our management were great at finding little ways to motivate us. I'd say they used every psychological trick in the book in those few days between games. I remember Fergal, in particular, highlighting all the talk about Paddy Curran's performance after the first game. Curran had been the star of the show and came away with eight points, more than half of Kerry's 15-point total.

'Kerry didn't play for 40 minutes lads… and they still got a result,' Fergal and his backroom would say. 'If they show up next week, they'll blow ye away!'

They were throwing down a gauntlet for us. There was no chance of us becoming complacent or taking anything for granted. We knew the size of the task that faced us, but we still believed we could bring a fourth All-Ireland minor title back to the county.

Once again, our preparation was excellent. I remember being in the Hyde and spending about an hour and a half on kickouts… and working through our positioning for breaking balls. Part of my job was to go up and break the ball to prevent the Kerry players from getting clean possession. There was a lot of work on details, like how Paul Gleeson would deal with Curran and the other match-ups across the pitch. They had playmakers in every line, so we spent a lot of time on that.

We also did a lot of work with two army guys in The Curragh around dealing with set-backs. 'What happens if we concede an early goal?'

'How do we respond to going behind?'

We were very well drilled by the end of that, and I don't think there was any eventuality that would have impacted on us executing our own game-plan. The preparation gave everyone confidence and removed some of the uncertainty when we did go out onto the pitch. The work we did that week meant there were fewer nerves as we paraded around the pitch next to the Kerry boys just before throw-in.

I had a very specific, and some would say daunting job… I had to mark Tommy Walsh and make sure he didn't win clean possession. Part of my role was to try and push him away from the play. Keep him out on the periphery, where he couldn't affect the game as much as he did at Croke Park the first day out. The big thing for us was to get on top of the likes of Walsh, Curran and David Moran. We had a saying, 'Hammer the hammer', and we had to impact their overall confidence so that they couldn't get going. Keep in mind, this was a Kerry team used to dictating the play so we'd no choice really but to be spot on in our preparation.

It's easy to say now but I wasn't overly happy with my performance in the replay! I got off to a good start, kicking a long-range free, which was good because I was 50-50 about going for it so early on. It was just on the '45' and it probably wasn't the ideal free to be hitting as my opening attempt. I did miss a few after that… I think I hit about three wides in that first-half. But I was happy enough with my contribution in open play in that I wasn't allowing Walsh to dominate in the air.

I won the first couple of kickouts so that was positive, but I did miss those first-half chances and also a goal chance in the second-half. In terms of my overall or nett contribution, I was happy. It was a different type of game from the first day. It was a messier game really and it was all about work rate, winning your individual battles around the pitch, and picking off scores whenever you could.

David O'Gara's goal that day was vital. We were a bit lucky actually that we got the bounce of the ball. It also came in a crucial period of the game, just after half-time. It was quite tight with about 10 minutes to go, and we missed chances, but thankfully we managed to convert a couple to go four points up. We felt we needed to be at least a couple of scores ahead for that bit of an insurance policy against such a formidable team.

There's an image of me at the full-time whistle, jumping in the air with a look of half-joy, half-relief. It was a huge thing being able to close out a game of that importance against such a good team. We felt we deserved it after getting the better of them in a lot of the key positions. It's hard to describe the feeling at the end when you know the mission is complete.

We had been under a bit of pressure in the closing stages even with a four-point lead. Kerry had won a long-range free, but we could see our supporters already lining up on the sideline ready to run in. You're desperately trying to keep your head but at the same time there's this little voice telling you, *There's no way we can lose this now… time's up.*

It was just a massive sense of relief when that final whistle blew. The work was done. We were All-Ireland champions, the first of our kind in Roscommon for 55 years. No one could take that away from us. We didn't have to go fighting for it anymore, there were no more training sessions… the cup would be coming back home with us! It's probably the wrong way of looking at it but I was fired on by the fear of losing rather than the joy of winning. We'd made it through the round robin and all the knockout stages, and just desperately wanted to get over the line. Could you imagine blowing your one chance of winning an All-Ireland title? Thankfully we wouldn't have to!

The presentation gave us some time with our families, and I got to see my parents, brother and sisters, uncles, cousins and everyone else. There were a lot of special memories made that day, particularly with my late father, Donie Snr. There's obviously a big family tradition when it comes to Roscommon GAA and Clann na nGael, so to get the opportunity to win an All-Ireland with dad watching on was just… well, seeing how proud he was is something that I'll never forget. It's a memory I can carry with me for the rest of my life. That in itself made it all worthwhile.

Watching my clubmate and good friend, David Flynn lifting the cup as captain was also a very special moment. David and I spent a lot of time together travelling to and from training and matches over the years. He is a real leader and has a very positive influence on his teammates. He's always someone you'd want on your side when things get tough.

And then there was the bus trip back to Roscommon with the Tom Markham Cup in tow. Not too many teams have made that journey. Not too many of them would have taken so long getting back either! We were stuck in traffic most of the way, but it was well worth it when we arrived in the Square in Roscommon town to be welcomed home by thousands of our supporters…

It was a truly magical occasion and I'm honoured that I got to be part of it!

CATHAL CREGG

ROSCOMMON 0-14 ★ SLIGO 0-13
Connacht SFC Final
MacHale Park, Castlebar
JULY 18, 2010

★ **ROSCOMMON:** G Claffey; S McDermott, P Domican, S Ormsby; C Dineen, S Purcell, D Casey (0-1); M Finneran, K Mannion; D Keenan (0-1), D O'Gara (0-1), **C Cregg (0-1)**; J Rogers, D Shine (0-10), G Heneghan. **Subs:** K Higgins for J Rogers, C Garvey for D Casey, J Dunning for D O'Gara, P Garvey for C Dineen.

★ **SLIGO:** P Greene; C Harrison (0-1), N McGuire, R Donovan; K Cawley, B Philips, J Davey; T Taylor, S Gilmartin; A Costello (0-5), M Breheny (0-2), E O'Hara; C McGee (0-1), A Marren (0-3), D Kelly. **Subs:** E Mullen for Taylor, K Sweeney for McGee, S Davey (0-1) for Gilmartin, N Ewing for Philips, S Coen for Breheny.

66

I FIRST BROKE into the senior set-up just before the 2006 National League campaign. I was playing with the under-21s, and senior manager, John Maughan called me up for a couple of A versus B games because they were short a few players. I must have impressed because he kept me on and gave me my debut as a half-time substitute against Limerick down in the Gaelic Grounds. My championship debut arrived in New York that summer, and I would later come on against Galway at the Hyde that year too. Then I made my first full start against Meath in the qualifiers in Navan. It was a pretty full-on first year!

There was a big 'changing of the guard' in the senior squad around that time and that probably gave me the opportunity to win a place on the panel. I was only out of minors at the time, so I don't know whether I'd have got in if there hadn't been such a big turnover of players. I suppose I got to test myself and develop

THE ACTION

★★★★★

THE YEAR OF 2010 was the ultimate 'mixed bag' for Roscommon football as the senior team was relegated to Division Four of the National League before the under-21s claimed Connacht glory. Outside the county, the Connacht senior final in MacHale Park that year was seen as very winnable for Sligo as the Rossies, with just three wins all year in league and championship football, faced off against the a talented Yeats side who had already sent the so-called 'big two' of Mayo and Galway crashing out of the championship.

Man of the Match Donie Shine, fresh from that underage success earlier in the year, kicked 0-10 from points and play and could have had even more. It was very much a Roscommon performance built on grit, determination and selfless teamwork. Everyone in Primrose and Blue played their part.

Trailing by six points at half-time, Sligo did finally get their act together in the second-half and produced an onslaught which looked destined to deliver the pre-match favourites the Nestor Cup. Roscommon, however, stuck to their task and two late, great points from Shine ultimately proved crucial in delivering another provincial success for Fergie O'Donnell's men.

Roscommon's first Connacht win in nine years, coming less than a month after the death of the county's most famous son, Dermot Earley, was met with unconfined joy, relief and perhaps a feeling of vindication by the Roscommon players, supporters and captain turned manager, Fergal O'Donnell.

★★★★★

when things weren't quite as competitive. Nowadays, it's hard for lads to come in when the team is competing at the level they are in Division One. If you make mistakes at that level, then you're found out straightaway.

The game has gone very physical now and this has resulted in lads not making their senior debuts until they're 21 or 22. There wasn't such a major focus on strength and conditioning back in 2005-06, if I'm honest. I do remember doing two years of weights over the winter as a minor with Tommy Craddock at the Community Centre in Kilbride. We were probably one of the first counties to do that at the time. Tommy came in with the seniors in 2006 in my first year. That type of training was slowly becoming more popular, probably due to what we were seeing from the more physical Ulster teams. Counties were doing bits and pieces, but they weren't doing it in a formal way. It's a given now that everyone does it from under-15s, and most counties now have their own performance coaches.

While I was breaking into the senior panel, the man who would later become our manager in 2010 was leading the county's minor team to All-Ireland glory. Make no mistake, Fergal O'Donnell was very good. He was demanding... but in a good way. He was a strong man-manager and very good to talk to one on one. He needed to be in 2010 too...

Our National League campaign that year was a disaster. We were relegated from Division Three with just one win from seven games, a one-point win over Louth. Our six defeats came against finalists Antrim and Sligo, Wexford, Cavan, Offaly and Fermanagh.

Thankfully, our championship campaign was a completely different story. Looking back, we got the maximum out of ourselves when it really mattered that year, particularly on Connacht final day and for the All-Ireland quarter-final against Cork. We left everything on the pitch on both of those days and I think a lot of that was down to Fergie. His preparation and attention to detail was legendary. I also found him very easy to work with... even if he was pushing you to your limits!

'We need to have everyone going in the right direction,' he'd always say.

It was the first time that I, and I'm sure most of that group, got into such an impressive physical condition. We trained very hard that year, even throughout a turgid league campaign when we weren't playing well. We'd train Tuesdays,

Thursdays, Saturdays… and even some Sundays, and we also went away for a couple of training camps. We'd spend hours training down in The Curragh and we also went to Wexford a couple of times. It wasn't all physical work either… there was lots of focus on general health and nutrition, flexibility and mobility work too.

You were probably doing something almost every day, but it wasn't that you were running yourself into the ground each time. On recovery days, you'd be doing bits of flexibility and mobility, which might only be 40 minutes of stretching in front of the telly, but it was still work that had to be done.

Martin McIntyre, who's been involved with Mayo the last number of years, was our sports science guy at that time. He was top notch, and he had the Sports Medicine background as well. We also had Niamh Fitzpatrick with us for the sports psychology side of it too. That was the first time we'd really done anything like that. I thought Niamh was excellent and she still is, to be fair.

There was a lot of one-to-one stuff and I think that's where it's at in terms of sports psychology. I don't think it really works in bigger groups because you have such a broad range of different age groups and backgrounds. You could have anywhere from an 18-year-old in a county senior panel, right up to a 35-year-old. They're just at completely different stages of their lives. Even two 25-year-olds could be at different junctures, so I think it's best to deal with them individually.

Over those couple of years, we did a lot of work on all that. Niamh had originally been with the Wexford hurlers when they'd broke through in 1996 and then went on to work closely with Olympians. There's no doubt she was a very important part of the set-up. I have a feeling that even when Fergal was pushing the boundaries in training sessions, he was tic-tacking with her on what he could and couldn't get away with!

I remember we had a big sit-down meeting after we were relegated that year. It was a frank and honest enough chat about our prospects, I can tell you! But in fairness to Fergal and the backroom team, they could see the work we were putting in. It was savage. We used to train on the back field in Ballyforan on Tuesdays… Jesus, there were some tough nights up there! I remember sloshing through the puddles of water in the middle of the field, being pushed to our absolute max. Fergal was good in how he framed it to keep us going.

'This WILL pay off', he'd tell us. But I'm not sure how many of us believed him on those wet winter nights running through the muck and puddles in Ballyforan.

Fergie's motivational strategy must have worked, however, because we were itching to get back out onto the pitch following that dismal league campaign. We wanted to put the relegation behind us and prove that we were good enough to represent Roscommon. There were a couple of challenge games lined up for us against the likes of Clare and Limerick. Those games, while ultimately meaningless, were good for our confidence ahead of the provincial championship.

We began our Connacht campaign that year in London, where we had a good 0-14 to 0-6 win. A lot of people mightn't have thought that was such a big deal at the time, but it certainly was for us. It was another building block after the confidence we'd gained from those earlier challenge games.

Without being disrespectful, our route to the Connacht final that year helped us a great deal. Relegation had dealt a big blow to our confidence, so it definitely suited us to build slowly, rather than be thrown to the wolves in Salthill or Castlebar.

The semi-final against Leitrim was another important step along the way. We had a decent five-point win, and I scored two points from play. The way we were playing now, there was more of a defensive structure about us. Myself and David Keenan would come back down the field to help out. I played the league at No 6 – it was role I'd played a lot for Western Gaels and at underage, so I was familiar with it. I had also played one year at wing back and a year as corner-forward at minor level. I'm not sure they knew where to put me!

The team was evolving with each game as we went through Connacht and, suddenly, we found we were conceding fewer scores. I think too that the under-21s coming back in helped. They were a seriously talented bunch and won Connacht that year. They lost out in the All-Ireland semi-final to the eventual winners Dublin, who had Jim Gavin in charge of them at that stage and Dean Rock leading the line. Lads like David Keenan, Donie Shine, Paul Garvey and Kevin Higgins came into the panel and brought that confidence from winning a provincial title with them.

Normally, nerves weren't really a thing for me because I felt like I prepared so well for matches. That hadn't always been the case, however. Before Fergal took over, my preparation would not have been anywhere near the level required for county football. But I would have bought into the sports psychology that year and I also brought my recovery and nutrition on to the next level. When I was younger, I would have probably looked down on a lot of that stuff. In 2010, I embraced it.

The final against Sligo was one of my better performances in a Roscommon jersey. I was marking Keelan Cawley for a while and then moved on to Johnny Davey. I was playing that defensive role and I was getting on a lot of breaking ball. I was in the zone. There's a bit of luck involved but it's also down to the timing of the tackle too. You just have to go for it… it's not the sexiest part of the game, but it's crucial.

I was playing the role of link man. Get on breaking ball, move it forward… start the next attack. Geoffrey Claffey was finding me with his kickouts, particularly in the second-half down underneath the stand in MacHale Park. It was a bit of mismatch height-wise with a couple of Sligo lads and that worked in my favour. We started attack after attack down my side of the field, with the Roscommon supporters roaring us on from the stand.

While I was happy with my defensive output it was also nice to be involved in the more glamorous side of football too. I chipped in with a point, but it was Donie Shine who led the way that day with 10. He had a serious game and kicked some outrageous scores.

Things were going to plan for us. The way we were set up frustrated Sligo and they got off to a slow start. It didn't help them that we were on it from the very first minute. They finally made a burst in the second-half and the game got tighter and tighter as the half wore on. But we stuck to our task and forced Sligo to kick a couple of wides under a lot of pressure.

I don't ever remember being too worried about the result but that was probably because of the belief we had going into the game. It helped that it was all panning out the way we were told it would too.

We were ahead by a single point at the full-time whistle and, suddenly, relegation to Division Four was a distant memory. It was madness out on the field. It was similar to beating Mayo in Castlebar in 2019 in terms of the scenes with the supporters afterwards.

Something that was said on the radio a couple of days before the match stuck with me. I think it might have been Martin Carney who said it… 'Roscommon gate-crash other teams' dreams'… or something like that anyway! We had our own dreams, of course, but that day felt like a really well-planned ambush. Outside of our group no one had expected us to pull it off and that made it all the sweeter.

Something came into my head at the full-time whistle, a memory from earlier on in the year. It was a really horrendous night up in Ballyforan, a night when you're questioning your sanity. Fergal turns and says to me, 'We'll beat Sligo in the Connacht final this year'. Sligo were on the same side of the draw as Mayo and Galway. Now I was questioning his sanity!

The pitch afterwards was swarmed with ecstatic Roscommon supporters and the dressing-room was some craic too. Coming back home on the bus through Ballinlough, Castlerea, and up into Roscommon… you're trying to take it all in your stride but, in reality, you can't really believe what's going on!

Sligo would have been hot favourites going into that Connacht final but we would have been bullish enough about our chances amongst ourselves. Both counties would always fancy a crack at each other. Certainly, any time I've come up against Sligo it's always been nip and tuck. They had beaten Mayo and Galway that year. They beat Mayo by four points! It's hard to imagine a tougher Connacht campaign for a Sligo side, in fairness, but they'd a right good team and were playing Division Two by then. They were the reason the final wouldn't feature Mayo or Galway for the first time in over 60 years.

So why didn't they win?

Well, I think it just all came together on the day for us. In terms of performance, I don't think there was anyone who put in a less than an 8 out of 10. There was a firm belief there that we could beat Sligo and that was down to all that hard work we'd put in throughout a difficult league campaign. Fergie was right, it *did* pay off!

As a manager he was unbelievable at putting the collective right at the centre of everything. Maybe that's why everyone was pushing on so much, even the lads who were just outside the team or match-day panel. In other teams I've played with, those lads would get annoyed that they weren't getting any game time… which is totally understandable. But in Fergie's teams there was none of that. Everyone was focused on the one cause. I don't really know how he did it, but I think it went back to those one-to-ones and the sports psychology. I just think he was top-class man manager too.

Everyone going in the one direction.

Our year sadly came to an end in the All-Ireland quarter-final against Cork that year. From my memory, we went a point up through Ger Heneghan with 55 minutes played in that game but then they brought three or four All Stars off the bench, and we couldn't live with them. They were a brilliant team. They'd won a couple of league titles and ultimately went on and won the All-Ireland that year. But you'd still have to be proud of the effort our lads put in. It just wasn't enough on the day.

A good few people still ask me whether I miss being out on the pitch. I go to the majority of games, bar a couple that are too far away because the kids just aren't at a good age to be bringing in the car! I can honestly say that I've never had the feeling that I wanted to be out there. By the end, I'd just had enough of it. Now, don't get me wrong, I enjoyed every bit of it ... but in my last year it had become more of a struggle.

When I was younger, I was usually in the zone in terms of preparation, playing and training, but Covid-19 came along and took me out of it. It had been a lifestyle up to that and everything from training to nutrition and recovery was bang on. There was a routine to it. When Covid came I got out of that routine. Inter-county football is a lifestyle... eat properly, do your recovery on a Monday, training on Tuesday, gym on Wednesday... you tick them all off the list each week.

But when you're stuck at home for a couple of months... well, you end up sitting down for a few nights here and there and watching TV or Netflix. I never really watched much telly before Covid and it wasn't down to laziness... I swear! You just fall out of that routine.

I really couldn't say anything negative about my time with Roscommon. Obviously, you look back and you'd like to have achieved a bit more, but I look back on those years very fondly. There were so many good times and it brought so many good things into my life.

I couldn't but thank everyone who was part of it alongside me.

SENAN KILBRIDE

ST BRIGID'S 0-13 ★ NEMO RANGERS 1-8
All-Ireland Club SFC Semi-Final,
Gaelic Grounds, Limerick
FEBRUARY 26, 2011

★ **ST BRIGID'S:** P Martin; R Kelly, D Donnelly, D Sheehy; I Kilbride (0-1), P Domican, G Cunniffe (0-1); G Dolan (0-1), K Mannion (0-1); E Sheehy (0-1), C McHugh, D Dolan (0-1); D O'Connor, **S Kilbride (0-6)**, F Dolan (0-1). **Subs:** Conor McHugh for Cathal McHugh, D Kelleher for O'Connor.

★ **NEMO RANGERS:** B Morgan; C O'Shea, D Kavanagh, A O'Reilly; C O'Brien, B O'Regan, D Breen; D Niblock, P Morgan (0-1); A Cronin, P Kerrigan, B O'Driscoll (0-1); J Masters (0-6), S O'Brien (1-0), D Kearney. **Subs:** D Mehigan for Kearney, W Morgan for O'Brien, A Morgan for O'Driscoll.

ST BRIGID'S HAD come off a couple of poor years in 2008 and '09 in the county after winning senior titles in 2005, '06 and '07. I guess we had taken our foot off the pedal for a while but by 2010 we had definitely regrouped. Noel O'Brien had come in as manager with Ger Paul Cunniffe and Michael O'Brien as selectors. It was always great to have local lads in charge of the team. They know the players, they know the club, and they bring a huge amount of passion, drive and energy to the job. It matters more to them.

There was a realisation among the panel that we had an opportunity to go and do something very special. Even when we won the county title back, the feeling around the club was, *We've been here before, it's time to push on now.*

No Roscommon club had ever won an All-Ireland senior title, but we had had a taste of provincial success in 2006 when we beat Corofin thanks to Karol

THE ACTION

★★★★★

SINCE WINNING THEIR seventh Roscommon SFC title in 2005, St Brigid's had been on a mission to reach the pinnacle of Connacht and then All-Ireland club football. Two more county titles followed after that first success in eight years, before a barren two-year spell which prompted some soul-searching at the Kiltoom club.

It wasn't long, however, before they were back at the top of the Connacht football tree, winning the county and provincial titles in 2010. The next step for Noel O'Brien's charges was a serious crack at the All-Ireland senior club title.

Nemo, of course, remain the undisputed kings of club football with seven All-Ireland club titles to their name, but in 2011 they met a St Brigid's team on the up.

Playing with the wind, Brigid's trailed 1-4 to 0-5 at half-time, thanks in part to a rather fortunate Sean O'Brien goal. The Roscommon side were transformed in the second-half, however, with Frankie Dolan dropping back to act as a link man and Man of the Match Senan Kilbride hugely influential from frees and play.

The situation did look precarious with just six minutes remaining, however, when Alan Cronin put Nemo 1-8 to 0-10 ahead, but a superb Gearoid Cunniffe score and an insurance point from Kilbride ensured that this dogged St Brigid's outfit qualified for their first ever All-Ireland senior club final, much to the delight of their supporters who had travelled to Limerick in big numbers.

★★★★★

'Mango' Mannion's wonder goal. Fast-forward to 2010, we had set out our stall out after winning the county final. We said we'd give it our all to get through the Connacht Championship that year and give the All-Ireland series a good rattle too, and that's exactly what we did.

There was also a feeling that we'd make it to the All-Ireland series before and not exactly done ourselves justice. This time around though things felt slightly different. We knew we had a very special group of players, but there was also the cold realisation that we'd have to put our heads down and target an All-Ireland title before that team was past its prime. There weren't too many teams around Roscommon speaking openly about winning All-Ireland titles back then… but we certainly were.

The build-up to our All-Ireland semi-final against Nemo Rangers is something I'll never forget. We had a few really tough months of training led by Mick O'Brien. He certainly seemed to enjoy putting us through our paces in the rain and the muck down on the back field in Kiltoom!

We had a lot of work done at this stage, and my teammates deserve great credit for taking ownership. Each of us felt responsible for maintaining our style of play throughout games and showing real leadership on the pitch. The likes of Mango, my brother, Ian, and Niall Grehan really stood up to be counted around this time too. Our forwards, myself included, also realised the importance of having the experienced Frankie Dolan playing with us. His range of passing was second to none in the country. He made us all look good really and when he was around our forward line played better. Frankie could find gaps no one else really could. All those guys led the team with strong, clear communication and that encouraged everyone to step up a level or two during those few months.

The task ahead of us couldn't have been much more difficult. We were drawn against Cork's Nemo Rangers, the most successful club in the history of Gaelic football at that time and still now. The underdogs' tag didn't faze us though; we actually relished it to be honest. We had watched Nemo play Dr Crokes in the Munster final, and they looked very strong. They got a couple of goals that day and it was obvious who their danger men were. They had the likes of James Masters and Paul Kerrigan, and they played a very pacy and skilful brand of football. Kerrigan must have been the fastest player in Ireland at the time.

While we knew we'd be up against it in taking on a real footballing powerhouse, we also took confidence in the fact that we had all that work done. Between those gruelling sessions in Kiltoom and the tough challenge games we had leading up to the semi-final, our lads wouldn't be found wanting in the Gaelic Grounds in Limerick. One of the biggest things that sticks out in my mind about that day is the outrageous support we had in the ground. It was simply unbelievable.

Pre-match nerves only really started affecting me towards the end of my career, when I realised time was running out. But from playing with Roscommon and the club at a high level, I had received sound advice from a variety of different people. We were always told to 'control the controllables'. Basically, can you control what the opposition do? No. Can you control the weather? Also no.

So, what exactly *is* in your control? Your own workrate. If you concentrate on that, the other things should fall into place.

Some players like to get really fired up before a game but that never really worked for me. I wanted to remain calm and focused on each play. That might have made me seem a bit laid-back at times, but I always tried to play with as much aggression as I could, while also maintaining composure. There's a thin line you have to walk between fighting for every ball and then being able to bring your heart rate under control, steady yourself, and take your chances.

The tight high-stakes games were the ones I really looked forward to. There's something special about battling alongside lads you grew up with to win glory for your local club. You had to do your own job up front while also doing your bit for your teammates by putting in a proper shift. It's no good just scoring points, you also have to get your fair share of tackles and blocks in too. There's also the added bonus that if you do manage to turn ball over, you're closer to the goal when you win possession... and your marker is out of the game.

We played with the wind in the first half in Limerick. It felt like a four- or five-point wind due to the strength of it. But with the unpredictable Irish weather, it didn't quite pan out that way...

There were a number of issues that day. Cathal McHugh went off injured pretty early in the game, and we struggled to work the ball into scorable positions. If it wasn't for lads pulling out some inspirational scores – including Ian from the left half-forward position – we would have been in a much worse position at half-time. As it was, we were behind 1-4 to 0-5, thanks mainly to a soft Nemo goal.

The scores may have been hard to come by in the opening 30 or so minutes, but we made sure we defended well at least. Nemo's goal came after just 12 minutes or so. There was a bit of luck involved in it too because I don't think Masters meant to drop his line-ball short. It landed in near the small square and Sean O'Brien just glanced it in. But we didn't let our heads drop and our intensive conditioning work began to show.

They had very few clear shooting opportunities after that. Our lads did a good job in keeping their potential danger men quiet too. Peter Domican was on Paul Kerrigan and stuck to his task well. Darragh Sheehy was on James Masters, and limited him to frees.

Despite our best efforts, we were still behind at half-time and playing against the breeze in the second-half, so we knew we'd have to knuckle down and prepare for a really tough 30 minutes.

Noel O'Brien spoke well at the break. The message from management and the leaders in our team was the same and very clear.

It was time to do ourselves justice.

Karol Mannion had a huge influence at half-time, and in that second-half. He was a real leader in the dressing-room. He was the one who kept us all composed and calm while driving home the important messages in a constructive and positive way. He was very level-headed. We were lucky that we had a few players like that in the group. There were also other players who led by example. They weren't ones for big speeches, but they let their own performances do the talking for them.

As a forward in a game like that you just have to remain patient. My dad always used to say, 'Defenders have to win every ball, but you only have to win one'. That's always stuck in my head when things aren't going to plan or maybe I'm going through a quiet spell. One ball might be the changing of the game, so it's important not to let the head drop or you might miss it.

If you're struggling to impose yourself on a game, then just work your way into it with a tackle, or by trying to get your hands on the ball in a simple way. It's about settling the nerves and trying to get the basics right until you get a chance to do what the team needs you to do, which is put the ball over the bar.

I was being picked up by Derek Kavanagh that day, who was also playing full-back for Cork. I just remember him being very strong and I didn't get many opportunities to really take him on. Not that he would have been the easiest man to go past anyway! Speed was never really my thing; the scores I got were usually down to quick turns or kicking the ball over my shoulder.

Something definitely turned for me in that second-half. I'm not sure what it was but I just threw my boot at any chances that came my way and the ball sailed over the bar. It's a great feeling when it clicks like that.

Overall, it was a tough battle against Kavanagh though and he definitely had the better of it in the first-half. Thankfully, there were more opportunities coming my way in the second-half and I seemed to have a bit more luck too, which always helps. To get those opportunities though you have to rely on your teammates to provide you with quality ball, and I was very lucky in that I was surrounded by talented players in every position. We also had an honest and hard-working team so I knew the chances would eventually come my way.

You don't play in an All-Ireland semi-final at any level and expect it to be easy, however. Nemo defended really well, and that forced me to pull a shot or two, but then you get a free or something and gain confidence. There's no doubt the nerves got the best of us in the first-half but there was no way we were going to continue in that vein in the second-half.

The message was loud and clear:

We're not lying down here lads.

We went up a few levels after the break and brought huge aggression and tenacity into the game. The breaks started going our way too; their midfielder David Niblock was sent off less than 10 minutes in. That was a huge slice of luck for us and one we made sure we took full advantage of.

Overall, I think we played well. Sure, it wasn't free-flowing attacking play, but we restricted them to just 1-8... a remarkable scoreline when you think of the talent they had. I think just 1-2 of that was from play too. You would have got long odds on that following their win over Dr Crokes.

It was all down to our ferocity in the tackle and the confidence we had in stamping our will on the game. The way we dominated midfield in that second-half was a collective effort, from half-backs to midfielders and half-forwards, everyone played their part. You have to earn the right to be able to move the ball into scoring positions, and we did that.

There was still that strong breeze to contend with… but we were in flow now and most of the shots just seem to pick up pace and drop nicely over the bar.

It was right to the end. They kicked a couple of nice scores and even took the lead at one stage to put the pressure back on us. But I remember Gearoid Cunniffe, one of the best strikers of a ball at the club, came up with a beautiful score, and I got a couple too to settle us down. We just about managed to see it out in the end, but we didn't care as long as we won.

There were some great scenes at the final whistle. Our supporters were going absolutely nuts thinking ahead to an All-Ireland final at Croke Park. We were exhausted but elated out on the pitch. It was so satisfying to come out in that second-half and turn things around. Everyone was buzzing.

We had finally pushed on from Connacht. It was one of the special days for St Brigid's. We now knew we could compete with the very best teams in the country. Nemo were a huge scalp, but also a very important stepping stone on our years-long journey to win an All-Ireland.

We'd had a taste of this before in 2007 when we ran into Crossmaglen in Mullingar. To be fair, I don't think the 1-11 to 0-11 scoreline properly reflected the Ulster champions' dominance that day. They were a different level, and that game was an important milestone in helping us realise what we needed to do as a group to reach that level.

Everyone still has such fond memories of that win over Nemo Rangers. The crowd was unbelievable that day and it was great seeing how happy our family was afterwards – mam, dad and all my friends from around the parish. It was just a really special day and I think everyone realised the significance of it too. There really was nothing better than soldiering with lads from your own parish and reaching an All-Ireland final. It was a huge day in the club's history too. Anyone I was speaking to on the pitch that day or back at the clubhouse that evening could see we were heading towards something monumental and how significant that win over Nemo Rangers was.

I remember one rather surreal moment in the dressing-room afterwards. It was perhaps my first time to play that well in such a high-profile match and someone came in to tell me I was wanted outside for an interview.

'They're giving you Man of the Match.'

Feck it anyway!

I don't think I'd given many interviews at that stage. I just wasn't very comfortable talking about myself, so I turned to Michael O'Brien for advice.

'Ah just distract them with the usual bullshit … important day for the club… it means so much to us… that sorta thing.'

It was sound advice. If it wasn't for Mick I would have been babbling as usual and left looking a bit uncomfortable! It was much easier to turn the spotlight back on your teammates… and they certainly deserved it too.

That elusive All-Ireland win didn't quite materialise for us in 2011 either, but that day in Limerick against Nemo Rangers was a vital step towards us going on to finally lift the Andy Merrigan Cup two years later against Ballymun Kickhams. The Gaelic Grounds was where the final leg of the journey up those steps of the Hogan Stand began.

99

FRANKIE DOLAN

ST BRIGID'S 2-11 ★ BALLYMUN KICKHAMS 2-10
AIB All-Ireland Senior Club Football Final
Croke Park, Dublin
MARCH 17, 2013

★ **ST BRIGID'S:** S Curran; G Cunniffe, P Domican, J Murray; N Grehan, D Donnelly (0-1), R Stack; K Mannion (1-2), I Kilbride; D Kelleher, R Blaine (0-1), D Dolan; Cathal McHugh, S Kilbride (1-3), **F Dolan (0-4). Subs:** G Dolan for Kelleher; E Sheehy for McHugh; Conor McHugh for Blaine; D Kelleher for Darren Dolan.

★ **BALLYMUN KICKHAMS:** S Currie; Eoin Dolan, S George, Enda Dolan; A Hubbard, K Connolly (0-1), J Burke (0-2); J McCarthy, P McMahon (1-0); Davy Byrne, K Leahy, J Whelan (0-2); T Furman (0-2), D Rock (1-3), E Reilly. **Subs:** Derek Byrne for Leahy; C Weir for George; J Small for Reilly.

66

WE HAD BEEN knocking on the door of the All-Ireland Club Championship since 2011. That year we beat the Munster champions, Nemo Rangers in the semi-final down in Limerick and that set up a final against Crossmaglen at Croke Park. The Ulster side were the dominant force in club football at the time. They beat us that day by three points and the gap between us was significant, but that defeat was an important milestone for us because it showed us exactly where we were compared to the very best.

In 2013, we were drawn to play Cross again in the semi-final in Mullingar. We had some history with the Armagh side; they had also knocked us out of the All-Ireland series in 2007. We were hoping it would be a case of 'third time lucky' six years on.

The game itself seemed to go by in a blur. I was drained by the end of it, and

THE ACTION

★★★★★

ST BRIGID'S HAD BEEN building towards this monumental day for almost eight years following their return to the top of the Roscommon club football tree. Their 2005 county senior title was followed by two more in quick succession. Their Connacht club title win in 2006 whetted the appetite for more but they were forced to wait another 10 years for provincial glory, winning again in 2011 and '12. These successes opened the Kiltoom's horizons once more, but they came up against an All-Ireland winning juggernaut in the shape of Crossmaglen in 2011.

Fast forward to 2013, and the Roscommon and Connacht champions finally slayed the Ulster dragon, gaining sweet revenge with a dogged win over Cross' in their Mullingar semi-final. That set up another Croke Park showdown with Leinster champions, Ballymun Kickhams.

It was Kickhams who started brightest and they plundered an impressive total of 2-3 in the opening 10 minutes alone. That Ballymun only managed to score seven points to Brigid's 2-10 for the remainder of this final speaks volumes about the Connacht champions' recovery. Kilbride was instrumental in the Brigid's recovery, first scoring a 12th minute goal to spark the comeback and later laying one on for Man of the Match, Karol Mannion. Brigid's had gone in at the break trailing but by the 38th minute both sides were level on 2-7 apiece.

Then Brigid's' talisman, Frankie Dolan, took over proceedings.

★★★★★

it wasn't until I was being interviewed by Brian Carthy afterwards that I became aware of how significant the result was.

I was pleased with my own performance that day. I scored a goal and two points, and probably could have got a second goal too, but I was taken out as I went to take the shot. Thankfully, Conor McHugh was following up and he stuck it away instead. It didn't bother me how it went in... as long as we won! The result was the most important thing that day and there was a feeling among players, management and supporters that we had finally slayed the dragon and taken a massive step towards Roscommon's very first All-Ireland club title. The only danger now was that we had peaked in the semi-final, believing that the hard work had already been done.

Ballymun were the Dublin and Leinster champions so there was no way we'd get away with any complacency at Croke Park. They were as physical as Crossmaglen, but also had a few players who would play a huge role in Dublin's dominance at inter-county level over the next seven years. I was genuinely worried whether our lads' heads were right going into it. When you beat a team like Crossmaglen, you can fall into the trap of thinking the job is already done. *Was Mullingar an All-Ireland final for some of our boys?*

To make things worse, I had broken my finger during training in the lead-up to the final. I was in a lot of pain and would have struggled to make it through the Ballymun game if not for our physiotherapist, Pat Regan. Pat made a splint and a mould for the injured finger which reduced the mobility but allowed me to play. It wasn't ideal preparation, but I would have had no problem chopping the finger off if it meant playing in the biggest game of my career.

When Pat wasn't making me splints and moulds for my damaged fingers, he was busy dragging me to Mass in Ballybay Church on the day of the final! St Patrick's Day that year fell on a Sunday and our match at 3.45pm in Dublin. The whole parish was on edge that day, and none more so than Pat. He phoned me early that morning to check on the hand and then ended up calling down to the house.

'Come on Frankie... we'll go to Mass,' he said when he arrived at the door that day.

'Mass, Pat? Have you forgotten we have a match up in Dublin today?'

He wouldn't take no for an answer and so off we went to morning Mass. Every soul in the church that day must have been wondering what we were doing there when we slipped in the side door. We were due to be playing at Croke Park just a few hours later and here were looking for divine inspiration!

Former Dublin footballer, Paul Curran who would later go on to manage Clann na nGael, was over Ballymun at that stage – they had beaten Dr Crokes of Kerry in their semi-final. As much as we were looking forward to our second bite of the All-Ireland cherry, we knew it would be a massive battle.

It turned out to be a dreadful day for football. The ball felt like a bar of soap at times, and lads were slipping and sliding all over the place. As bad as the conditions were, our slow start is still difficult to explain. We were creating chances, but Ballymun were clinical every single time they got into scoring range.

They were on a roll in the opening 10 minutes and wiping the floor with us. They led by 2-3 to 0-1 and our supporters were probably beginning to fear the worst. We were just trying to hang on until the half-time whistle. It was a completely different game to the one against Crossmaglen. Our semi-final had been a slow, punishing brawl but this was real end-to-end stuff. The pace was unreal.

Just halfway through the first-half and we were already desperate for a goal to give us some sort of lifeline. But as well as being dangerous in attack, Ballymun had gone through the Dublin Championship without conceding a goal. They had even managed to put the shackles on the great 'Gooch' Cooper in the semi-final.

What they hadn't counted on were the performances of Senan Kilbride and Karol Mannion, who lit up a dark Croke Park that afternoon.

While we chipped away at their first-half lead, the north Dubliners were still dominating us around the middle of the park, and I remember Ronan Stack being sent out there to help put a stop to their constant raids. We were being over-run and I felt we needed to get my brother, Garvan on for the second-half. His physicality would be crucial if we wanted to have any chance of turning the tide.

By the time the whistle went to end the half, we had somehow managed to claw our way back to within four points. It must have been a terrific game to watch as Ballymun led by 2-6 to 1-5.

I remember sprinting back to the dressing-room and seeking out our coach Liam McHale. Manager Kevin McStay was still making his way down from the stand, where he had been overseeing the first-half. I found McHale in the toilets and even squeezed in beside him in a cubicle!

'Look Liam, we're getting killed in midfield. Ye have to bring Garvan on before this gets away from us.'

Things were a bit frantic when I walked back into the dressing-room. It later transpired that Kevin had got lost in the maze of elevators on the way down from the stand. Some of the senior lads such as Karol and Mark O'Carroll had spoken well when the lads had first arrived in at the break, but now there was too much talking going on and we were in danger of going down a rabbit hole.

Kevin was in the management room with the other members of the backroom by this point and Mango had gone in to tell them they needed to speak to us, because there were too many people talking.

Then Kevin and Liam came into us and rejigged things brilliantly. Garvan was brought on at midfield, and Ian Kilbride was pushed back to centre-back. Suddenly, there was far more physicality through the spine of the team.

The real masterstroke though was moving Darragh Donnelly from centre-back up to centre-forward. That changed the whole complexion of the game, and we played like a completely different team in the second-half.

We all lifted it a level too. A good indication of which team has the momentum is the breaking ball. We were much sharper to it in the second period and that allowed us to enjoy more control over the game.

Our full-back line was crucial in that second-half. The lads really got on top of Dean Rock and Ted Furman and frustrated the hell out of them. Shane Curran in goals played a vital role in that too. He was constantly in the ear of any player, official, supporter or anyone from Ballymun who would listen!

Cake might come across as a bit of a lunatic at times but he's also an incredibly intelligent goalkeeper. I have taken my fair share of slagging and abuse in my time, but I wouldn't have enjoyed playing as a forward for Ballymun that day. The constant mouthing can put you off your game, even for just a split second.

Peter Domican, Ronan Stack and my brother, Darren, deserve a mention for their performances in that second-half too. They were brilliant in and out of possession, but every single player played a part. It was much better all round and, without wanting to sound cocky, I felt that we could have won it with a bit more to spare in the end. The final few minutes were maybe a little bit more dramatic and nerve-racking then they needed to be, but winning was all that mattered.

While I scored the winning point at the very end, it was Senan Kilbride's goal in the first-half that proved to be the crucial score. It would have been almost impossible to rescue the situation in the second-half without it. Both he and Karol Mannion were unbelievable that day and Mango got a very clever goal too where he followed up on an attack and fisted the ball low into the ground. Those boys were the definition of 'big game' players.

As for the clinching point at the very end, well, I can still feel the hairs stand up on the back of my neck to this day. The tension was almost unbearable going into the closing stages. There was never more than a point in the difference and both sides were just waiting for the other team to blink. It really could have gone either way and neither side really deserved to lose it.

It came down to the very last possession of the game.

We had thrown away another easy chance and John Small took possession for Ballymun and raced down the wing… the Ballymun supporters roaring him on from the Cusack Stand. Thankfully, he mishit a hand-pass and allowed Niall Grehan to get his hand in and tap it loose.

Niall then tore out in front of Jason Whelan to complete the turnover and set us on our way towards the Canal end.

I can still hear that wave of St Brigid's' noise ringing in my ears. It seemed to carry the ball up the pitch, where it met Garvan at full tilt. He just managed to get his hand-pass away before being taken out.

The ball was fractionally short, and I was left with two options… either go towards the ball and get clobbered for a free, just inside Ballymun's half… or trust that the ball would skid up off the surface and make it through to me.

Luckily, it bounced into my hands as I vaulted over Conor Weir, who had been a fingertip away from winning possession back for Ballymun. It turned out to be the perfect pass in the conditions!

Looking back at the video today, I did well to keep my balance, steady myself and squeeze a shot off with my left foot as Ballymun defenders swarmed in. Croker wasn't full by any means but the noise around the place when that one went over was deafening. You could almost hear the relief from the St Brigid's' supporters.

The full-time whistle went shortly after that, and it was pure mayhem. There were bodies sprawled all over the place. The dejected Ballymun lads fell to the turf exhausted – a pain we knew all too well. The adrenaline had kicked in for us this time around as we were mobbed by the substitutes and backroom team.

Apart from the win over Crossmaglen in the semi-final, it was probably the best feeling I've ever had after a game of football. Sheer ecstasy.

That All-Ireland final was a credit to both sets of players. The conditions were poor but that only added to the drama, and the thrills and spills. We were both just intent on playing football. At the end, it was just sheer relief. When John Small advanced with the ball I feared the worst. Those were the fine margins between winning and losing.

Looking back, I'm convinced that the noise from our supporters carried us down the field like a wave. The cheers when we won the turnover seemed to create momentum with each phase of the move, ending in a huge roar when the ball went over the bar.

I had never experienced anything like those few seconds between winning possession and slotting it over. It's something that I'll never forget for as long as I live. Being on the pitch that day with my two brothers, Garvan and Darren, made it even more special.

Strangely, the celebrations felt slightly muted that day as we made our way up those 34 steps on the Hogan Stand. Maybe we really did feel we had done the hard work by finally getting the better of Crossmaglen in the semi-final. But I think it was because we knew how losing an All-Ireland final felt and didn't want to be rubbing Ballymun's noses in it.

You could see how much it meant to our loyal supporters though, particularly the older members of the club, who had had to watch our neighbours, Clann na nGael dominate in Roscommon and Connacht for years. It was very emotional talking to them afterwards and I became a bit overwhelmed when it finally sunk in that we had delivered a title that no other Roscommon club had ever won.

There was no singing or shouting in the dressing-room as we got changed afterwards, the Andy Merrigan Cup sitting there beside us. Kevin McStay came into the dressing-room and reminded us that we had to respect our opponents. Not that Ballymun would have heard us or anything, but we remained dignified anyway. We huddled together in the warm-up room with the cup in the centre of our circle. McStay gathered us around him for one more talk before heading home.

'Now men, as a group you may never be here again. Some of you will stop playing altogether and there's no guarantee that the rest of you will scale this mountain again. Some of you won't even see each other again for a number of years, but I can tell you for sure that you'll be at each other's funerals… hopefully many years from now'.

Kevin was hammering home his point that we had reached the peak and there were no guarantees that we'd ever get to repeat a day like that again. It was his way of bringing home to us the scale of our achievement and warning us to soak up the moment. His words would turn out to be prophetic in the years after 2013, but it was hard to believe the only way was down at that moment in Croke Park.

We all had one or two bottles of beer with the post-match dinner in Croke Park, but there was to be no alcohol on the bus back to Roscommon. That was down to Kevin, who was conscious that there would be young supporters there to welcome us home later that night.

It was a very sober but happy bus journey back to Roscommon.

We disembarked on the bridge in Athlone and walked the cup back across the Roscommon border. It was a great feeling to share that moment with the supporters. Then it was back to the Hodson Bay Hotel for a celebration and that's when the real craic started!

Everyone associated with the club was there that night, and even some who weren't, including the well-known singer songwriter, Phil Coulter. He was staying in the hotel for another engagement but that didn't stop Cake from dragging him in to perform for the new All-Ireland club champions.

After a meal and a few pints in the Hodson Bay, it was back to the club to continue the celebrations. I always enjoyed the days after a big win more. The texts usually went around on the Monday to arrange a team session somewhere in Athlone, Galway or Dublin. That Monday after the All-Ireland was no different… and we ended up at The Snug in Athlone.

The place was mobbed on account of it being a Bank Holiday and there were six of us who couldn't even get in the door. We decided to walk across the road to Seán's Bar where we could enjoy a few pints in comfort. From what I remember, the floor in The Snug had to be replaced soon after that session!

Looking back on that All-Ireland win, great credit must go to the likes of Noel O'Brien for the great work he'd done with the team prior to 2012. The foundations for our success were laid long before St Patrick's Day 2013 under managers such as John O'Mahony and Anthony Cunningham too. There was some great work done at the club in those years and it paid off in county and provincial titles and then, ultimately, with 'The Holy Grail'.

It was a historic day for the club against Ballymun and it was lovely that great clubmen like Jimmy Mannion, Pat Dennehy and the legendary Gerry O'Malley were there to see us win an All-Ireland title too.

The players made huge sacrifices to get us there, and they deserve a lot of credit for that. But it doesn't stop with them. Their families, including their parents and partners, had a huge part in it too. We had a strong, patient support network behind us that enabled us to compete at the very highest level for a number of years. They were all incredible and because of them we were able to challenge the very best teams in the country and then, finally, bring the All-Ireland Senior Club title back to Roscommon, and back to Kiltoom.

SEÁN McDERMOTT

ROSCOMMON 0-14 ★ KERRY 1-10

National Football League

Fitzgerald Stadium, Killarney

FEBRUARY 7, 2016

★ **ROSCOMMON:** D O'Malley; **S McDermott**, N Collins, N McInerney; D Murray, N Daly, R Stack; E Smith (0-3), I Kilbride; F Cregg (0-2), C Daly, C Devaney (0-2); C Murtagh (0-2), C Connolly (0-1), C Cregg (0-4). **Subs:** C Shine for Kilbride, S Purcell for C Daly, R Daly for C Cregg, C McHugh for Connolly.

★ **KERRY:** B Kelly; B Ó Beaglaoich, M Griffin, S Enright; P Murphy, A O'Mahony, K Young; D Moran, J Buckley (0-2); J Lyne; D O'Sullivan, D Walsh; BJ Keane (0-5), T Walsh (0-1), S O'Brien (1-1). **Subs:** T O'Sullivan for Lyne, A Fitzgerald for D Walsh, C Cox (0-1, 1 free) for Keane, F Fitzgerald for Enright, Barry O'Sullivan for Buckley, Brendan O'Sullivan for T Walsh.

IT WAS EXCITING times for Roscommon football in late 2015 because we had started to hear rumours that Kevin McStay would be managing the team the following year. We heard also that Liam McHale was going to be part of his backroom team and, if that wasn't impressive enough, it quickly became known that they wouldn't be taking the job without Fergal O'Donnell. This was really exciting to me, and I remember thinking, *With this management team, we are going places.*

I think that management line-up gave everyone goosebumps at the time, and I was certainly looking forward to the 2016 season. If I'm being honest, I didn't know an awful lot about Kevin or Liam at that stage, but I knew everything I needed to know about Fergie because he had managed the team from 2009 to '11. The work he had done back then had set him apart. I knew the type of fella

THE ACTION

★★★★★

IT WAS THE hosts who started the brightest and rattled off three unanswered points in the first eight minutes, but the Kingdom then went 19 minutes without a score, however, as Roscommon began to get to grips with them. The Rossies used the strong breeze to their advantage as they scored eight consecutive points to take control.

It was midfielder Enda Smith who opened Roscommon's account after 10 long opening minutes, before Cathal Cregg levelled matters after Donnachadh Walsh had struck the post for Kerry at the other end of the field. Cregg, Ciaráin Murtagh and Cian Connelly were causing the Kerry defence all sorts of problems as the visitors opened up a 0-8 to 0-3 lead with 25 minutes played.

However, the Kerry response was swift and brutal as points from BJ Keane, Tommy Walsh and a well-taken goal from Stephen O'Brien brought them level before a late Johnny Buckley score gave them a 1-6 to 0-8 lead at the interval.

It appeared the writing was on the wall for the Rossies early in the second-half as Kerry stretched their lead thanks to two Barry John Keane points but, apart from a 49th minute point from O'Brien, the Kingdom would only trouble the scoreboard on one further occasion... through a late consolation point from the now Roscommon forward, Conor Cox.

That second-half was all about Roscommon as they stormed to an unlikely victory, playing a swashbuckling style of football all too rarely seen in the modern game.

★★★★★

Fergie was and how much Roscommon meant to him. There would be no stone left unturned as we prepared for our first season in Division One in a long time.

Kevin, Fergie and Liam would be taking over the reins from Kerryman John Evans, who had taken the job in 2013 and led us to back-to-back promotions, catapulting us from Division Three to the top tier in just two seasons. I don't know if people really understand the work that John did for Roscommon football. I know that things didn't quite work out for us in the championship under him but the work he did from 2013 to '15 was absolutely extraordinary.

The reality of it was that the seasons were long and very intense, and we would have put an awful lot of work into our league matches in those years. It was difficult to maintain that level of intensity right the way through the year. But the people of Roscommon need to know that the work John did every year was absolutely phenomenal. He'll always hold a special place in my heart because he loved Roscommon football, and had a massive amount of belief in us.

That period between 2013 and '15 was what senior inter-county football is all about: moving up the divisions, getting back to Croke Park every year, and winning some silverware. When I started my career back in 2005, Roscommon football was in a very low place, and I remember there was a big turnover of players at the time. I was only a young lad of 20 or 21 years of age and probably knew no different. But to see what we achieved in 2014 and '15 was massive and, suddenly, we were going to be dining with the big boys of Gaelic football in Division One.

It was all very exciting.

You're certainly up against the *best of the best* in Division One but I have to say that no matter what county you go to there are top-quality corner-forwards and full -forwards. One of the best forwards I ever marked was actually a fella from Offaly, Niall McNamee. He was an absolutely outstanding footballer, right up there with the top three forwards I've ever played against. He may have played Division One football at some point in his career, I'm not sure, but he would have played most of his career in the lower divisions. So, that proved to me that the challenge in Division One was more about the preparation of the team because as a back, I was coming up against quality players in every game, whether it was Divisions Three, Two or One.

Against the best teams, it was all about how systems work; things like how you were set up defensively or how you dealt with both the opposition kickouts and your own. After that, you just had to have faith in what you were doing. I knew that with the management team we had in place for 2016 that the work was going to be done and that we were in safe hands.

Not that it got off to the best of starts…

We lost our first game that year at home to Monaghan in Kiltoom. It was a game we were winning throughout before they got a late point, and then Conor McManus grabbed a goal to win it right at the very end. It was harsh early lesson in what we could expect for the year ahead.

As if the challenge of staying in Division One wasn't daunting enough, we also lost home advantage that year because Dr Hyde Park was out of commission for most of the campaign. Our opening game was in Kiltoom and then we were forced to play Down in Longford. There was also the debacle around our last league fixture against Dublin, which was originally down for the Hyde and then moved to Carrick on the morning of the game following a deluge of rain the night before. The Mayo game at the end of March had gone ahead at the county ground, but the pitch was in a dreadful state by then. I think there was pressure on the county board to get games played in Roscommon, but the weather just never played ball.

In terms of preparation for that game against Dublin, in particular, that late move to Páirc Seán wasn't something we really passed any heed on as players. We arrived at The Abbey Hotel in Roscommon as usual and had already heard that the game would probably be moved to Leitrim. The pitch in Carrick was also touch and go because there had been torrential rain all over the country the night before.

We were six points down at half-time in that game, but we were much improved in the second-half. Ciaráin Murtagh was outstanding at 11 that day and Seán Mullooly came on for me after I was black carded, and he was brilliant too. Lads rolled up their sleeves and it was great to be able to showcase the ability we had against the reigning All-Ireland champions. It was another game that showed everyone, locally and nationally, that we were capable of competing in Division One, and despite losing to the Dubs, we had already done enough to stay there the following year too.

That round seven game seemed a long way off after our opening defeat to Monaghan, however, and things didn't get much easier for us in round two either… a trip to Fitzgerald Stadium in Killarney to take on Kerry!

We knew exactly what we were up against; it was a really daunting task, but we also knew we had a lot of quality. It was the best Roscommon panel that I have ever been involved with. I know we might have won a Connacht title the following year and played Division One in 2018, but without a shadow of a doubt, that year was the best group.

In preparation for the Kerry game, we stayed down the night before and landed in Fitzgerald Stadium an hour and a half before throw-in. There was no waiting around either. We went into the dressing-room, got ourselves ready, and out we went to a training pitch at the side of the stadium. I'll never forget that. It was like playing in a swamp, which made the warm-up interesting!

The nerves were up at this stage, and I think we were all thinking the same thing, *We could really do with something here.* Now obviously no one really expected us to get any sort of a result, but it turned out to be the game that set our league campaign off and running. It was also a game that really instilled confidence throughout our squad because before that game there were probably a few lads wondering, *Do we deserve to be here? Should we be playing at this level?* That was put to bed fairly firmly after that trip to Killarney.

Tommy Walsh was playing full-forward that day and Neil Patrick Collins had a fantastic game on him. Neil is a man we probably didn't see enough of in a Roscommon jersey, really. He was an outstanding talent and a born No 3. Cathal Cregg was outstanding too in the half-forward line. We also had some talented younger players coming through that year. Cathal Compton and Sean Mullooly were fairly new to the scene; you had the Dalys and David Murray, Niall McInerney from Brigid's, Ciaráin and Diarmuid Murtagh… most of them are household names now!

We also had players like Ian and Senan Kilbride, Cathal Cregg and Fintan Cregg, Conor Devaney, Geoffrey Claffey and me, who had a lot of experience. There was a great blend of youth and experience throughout the team, and winning that game really proved to lads that we deserved to play at that level.

The Kerry game was the evidence we needed, while the games after that showed everyone else what we were capable off. We went down to Cork in the next game and hit 4-25, and then our home game against Down was played in Longford and we won that by around 10 points too. Then the round five game against Donegal in Letterkenny was one in which we played some absolutely outstanding stuff. They were the four wins that guaranteed our safety that year, but they all followed on from that game in Killarney, when we really found our feet.

I was picking up Barry John Keane that night in Killarney. I was definitely nervous at the start of the game, but I became more comfortable as it went on. We knew we were in the game and that breathes confidence into everyone. You might watch a game and think, *They're very slow to get going*, and that can happen when lads are tentative or a bit nervy at the start. Then you get the first touch of the ball and the crowd get up for it, and you settle into the challenge.

As a defensive unit, we worked quite well that evening. David Murray was playing at 6 and he picked up Darran O'Sullivan and he did really well against him. I would have been very happy with my performance and my whole league campaign that year. I felt like I played very solid throughout and I suppose that's all you can do as a corner-back.

We had put a lot of work in early in the year and we were quite fit by the time we went down to Kerry. Where we further ahead of Kerry and some other teams at that stage? It's possible, but I don't really know. I think in a lot of the league games if one team wins then people will say, 'They've more work done'. That's just hearsay really; the team that wins always looks fitter because things went their way.

We were back on the horse fairly early at the start of 2016 because we knew playing in Division One that we'd have to have a bit more preparation work done compared with other teams who had that experience in the top flight. The result was that our fitness levels were through the roof. Keith Carr from Galway was our strength and conditioning coach. Keith had been involved with us under John Evans, and Fergal and Kevin were obviously impressed when they met him so kept him on board. That was no surprise to us because we knew he was top of his game. You could see it in us; we had added a lot of bulk but were still moving well across the ground. The work we had put in was obvious throughout that league campaign.

Overall, I think that league campaign was every bit as impressive as 2023. It was our first year back in Division One in quite some time, but it laid the foundations for Roscommon teams to become regulars there. For me personally, it was a real marker that said I deserved to be playing at this level, and that I was good enough. I always knew deep down in my heart that I was well capable of playing against the very best, so it was very special to play consistently at that level and particularly throughout 2016.

Unfortunately, the championship didn't go quite to plan that year. We were well beaten by Galway in the Connacht final after a replay, before bowing out disappointingly against Clare in the qualifiers. These things happen. To my mind, that year's league campaign was still the making of a number of players and the arrival of Roscommon as a real force.

In the years that followed, we spent a few seasons jumping between Divisions Two and One, but I've never seen that as a major problem really. As long as we were in the top eight or 10 every year, I think we could be happy enough with that.

One thing's for sure though, Roscommon is now more than capable of playing at the highest level, and being in Division One gives us a much better chance of developing players to the best of their ability. That exciting campaign in 2016 was the start of that.

CONOR DEVANEY

ROSCOMMON 2-15 ★ GALWAY 0-12
Connacht SFC Final
Pearse Stadium, Salthill
JULY 9, 2017

★ **ROSCOMMON:** C Lavin; D Murray, N McInerney, S McDermott; **C Devaney (0-3)**, S Mullooly, J McManus; T O'Rourke, E Smith; F Cregg, N Kilroy, B Stack (1-0); C Murtagh (0-3), D Murtagh (0-5), C Connolly (1-1). **Subs:** G Patterson for Murray, Murray for Patterson, I Kilbride for Cregg, D Smith (0-2) for D Murtagh, Colin Compton for C Murtagh, R Stack for Kilroy, S Killoran (0-1) for B Stack.

★ **GALWAY:** R Lavelle; C Sweeney, D Kyne, E Kerin; G O'Donnell (0-1), G Bradshaw, L Silke; P Conroy (0-2), F O Curraoin; T Flynn, E Brannigan, J Heaney; M Daly (0-1), D Comer (0-2), S Walsh (0-6). **Subs:** G Sice for Heaney, D Cummins for Brannigan, M Lundy for Flynn, E Tierney for O Curraoin, D Wynne for Conroy.

THAT YEAR WAS Kevin McStay's first full year in sole charge of the Roscommon senior team. It was the year after he and Fergal O'Donnell had taken charge of us and led us through a very good Division One campaign. Nothing had changed in terms of the feeling in the panel, but one thing that was different maybe was that there were fewer people involved in the backroom team.

There was definitely more of a relaxed approach under Kevin. He was great for players psychologically in that he would give you loads of confidence. In that sense, it was different because we were getting lots of messages from lots of different people the previous year. Not that that was a bad thing either! The level of detail we received about the opposition in 2016 was unreal. Neither approach was wrong, it was just more laid-back under Kevin and Liam McHale.

Liam, as everyone knows, likes to be the nice guy or 'Good Cop'. That's exactly

THE ACTION

★★★★★

IN WHAT WAS Roscommon's first championship win in Salthill since 1988, Kevin McStay's troops tore into Galway with fast attacking football, aided by the wind, in an opening quarter which yielded a 1-6 to 0-2 lead.

The highlight of the opening 35 minutes was Cian Connolly's superb finish to the net following a peach of a pass from Diarmuid Murtagh. It was advantage Roscommon at the break as they led by seven points.

On the resumption, it appeared as though the hosts and reigning Connacht champions were making good use of their wind advantage. Shane Walsh and Damien Comer points cut the gap to five within the first three minutes.

Then up stepped Brian Stack to put the game almost beyond doubt after 41 minutes. He collected a kickout, soloed towards the Galway goal, and finished to the net for his first championship goal. It was now 2-8 to 0-5 in favour of the Rossies and the game already looked over as a contest.

In front of their own shell-shocked supporters, Galway had no option but to keep going. Six points in succession threatened a grandstand finish before a Diarmuid Murtagh free stopped the rot. Further points from Cian Connolly and Donie Smith meant Roscommon led by 2-11 to 0-12 going into the last 10 minutes. The, by now wilting champions, had no further rallies, and they even failed to register a single score from the 54th minute to the full-time whistle.

★★★★★

what he is too. Preparation for games became more relaxed, and mostly about confidence building and focusing on our strengths. That would provide you with a big lift in the run up to matches.

While we had stayed in Division One in 2016, we lost the Connacht final after a heavy defeat to Galway in the replay at Castlebar. There was definitely a bit of a revenge mission element to 2017; we wanted to set the record straight after what happened in Castlebar. We were hammered the year before... it was pretty much over within 10 or 15 minutes. Now, some might say that was nothing new... there's been many a day in Castlebar, against a different team, when the game was over after 10 or 15 minutes!

It must be a psychological thing because I've always got a sense that we had every chance of beating Galway down the years, but with Mayo it's a different story. I don't know why that is? That was definitely the feeling in 2017, that, *Yeah, we're going to beat them.* I can remember that feeling even today. Everyone else in the panel must have felt that way too.

The final that year was in Salthill and one of the things Kevin did ahead of the game took a lot of players by surprise. He told us we'd be staying in The Abbey Hotel in Roscommon the night before. Usually, we would travel down a day in advance and stay in a hotel down there. At the time, I was renting a house across the road from The Abbey, but he insisted that we all stay in the hotel regardless! He felt it was the only feasible way of having us all together the night before. In hindsight, his plan worked!

Again, it was all about getting us relaxed and confident heading into a big game. Now, we weren't up in The Abbey all night having meetings about what to do with Damien Comer or talking about Johnny Heaney or anything like that. We had a quick meeting, talked about the game, and then went off to bed where you could chat more about the game with your roommate... if that's what you wanted. I just remember it as the only time I've ever had to stay with the team *in* Roscommon. That's the way Kevin was. He always had an idea or plan that he felt might be successful and he just went with it.

Another thing about Kevin was that he was fine motivator. I know there's infamous videos of some of his half-time talks going around but before the game it was all far more relaxed! It was usually Liam who would go around and make sure he spoke to everyone individually, usually on the morning of a game. We went to the Galway Bay Hotel when we got to Salthill that morning and he went around everyone, not just the starting 15, EVERYONE. Liam would always have a positive spin on things no matter what and he'd just fill you with loads of confidence.

I remember him saying to me, 'If you miss a shot from a position you'd normally score from, don't let it stop you from having another go'. His argument was that most players stop shooting if they have a bad wide, but it should be the opposite.

If you've missed four, you're hardly going to miss five...

That's just an example of how Liam looked at the game. It relieved some of the pressure knowing that he wouldn't mind if you missed a shot, provided it was within a reasonable range. It was just a different way of thinking and maybe something he brought with him from his basketball days.

I remember feeling calm and confident in Salthill, and just *knowing* that I was going to play well. I always liked playing against Galway and I just knew that day was going to go well for us.

Every time we played Galway, I was given the difficult task of marking Johnny Heaney. Now sometimes it would be me marking Johnny, and other times it would be Johnny marking me because we both varied between wing-back and wing-forward. I always felt marking Johnny that I'd get plenty of opportunities to get on the ball... perhaps he felt the same way about me!

The way Galway played then, and still play, they give you a lot of time to get on the ball and use it. Whereas if you played the likes of Tyrone you'd be thinking, *I might not see much of the ball here.* Whatever else was going to happen against Galway, at least you knew you'd get lots of possession. I was a wing-forward who could play a bit of football, so that's what I wanted and that's exactly what happened that day in Salthill.

Myself and Johnny always had good battles down through the years. I'm sure he'd agree, and he probably enjoyed playing against me as well. That day just happened to be one of those days when I had the better of it.

I remember the weather was absolutely horrendous that day in Salthill... as it seemed to be most of the time we played there. I know of a couple of supporters who stayed at the Galway Bay Hotel to watch the match on television rather than brave the walk down to the ground. I'm sure they later regretted that decision!

At half-time the feeling was that we were well able to go on and win the game. We knew what we were doing; we were finding it easy to get into scoring positions and believed we were well in control at that stage. I distinctly remember several players saying we could push on and win comfortably. That doesn't always happen with Roscommon, but it did that day. We had some really good players, and everything was just working out for us. It was just one of those days when not even the weather could stop us from playing our football.

I'd always be one for trying little things. Sometimes they work, sometimes they don't. But there was one phase of play I remember fondly from that game. I was being closed down by three Galway players but managed to chip the ball up off the ground and spun away from them in one movement. More often than not against a team like Galway you'd get hit or dispossessed, especially with a wet ball, but it just worked out and it started us off on another attack. It was just one of those days where everything went like clockwork.

At the full-time whistle I made sure to make a beeline for my then Roscommon Community College teaching colleagues, Tom Flynn and Paul Conroy. We had been talking about the game in work in the build-up, of course, so I made sure I went over to commiserate with them before joining in with the celebrations.

Paul is obviously still playing for Galway, and seems to be getting better and better as the years go on. Tom also had a few very big games for the footballers and the hurlers. Both were brilliant players. We had flagged Tom as one of their players who, if given time and space, could be very effective. John McManus had a very good game on him that day. He relished the task and whatever he did that day it worked, because Tom was kept quiet.

It was our first Connacht win since 2010 so obviously the celebrations were something else. We went back to the Galway Bay Hotel where most of our supporters had congregated before the game for breakfast. The place was absolutely thronged.

This might sound strange, but in the immediate aftermath of a game I wouldn't be an advocate of all the supporters coming onto the pitch at once. I just find it a bit overwhelming. After playing hard for 70 or 75 minutes, I just want to get over to the sideline, get some space and drink a bottle of water. The final whistle goes and suddenly you're surrounded by 10,000 fans, when you just really want a drink or to speak to someone in peace, like that day with Tom and Paul.

That's why winning at Croke Park – not that we've done that too often – is probably better for me because the supporters aren't usually allowed on the pitch afterwards. It means you can take your time, and go and pick family and friends out in the stand if you want to. I know that many supporters would completely disagree with this by the way, as rushing out onto the pitch is part and parcel of the excitement after a big win.

Later that night, we were back safely in Roscommon town, where we drove up Main Street and got off the bus to be met by thousands of supporters in the Square. The celebrations weren't a week-long event or anything like that... sure we were back training again that Tuesday night for an All-Ireland quarter-final. It was the Sunday night in Roscommon and the 'Monday Club' in Carrick but that was it as far as the celebrations went.

While I'm not a fan of the 'pitch invasion', standing up on the side of the trailer that night in the Square was okay. Once you've seen your family and you're back in Roscommon then, by all means, let the celebrations with the supporters begin. It's brilliant then; you're going from pub to pub and meeting everyone as you make your way up the town before predictably ending up in Rockfords like everyone else! That's the highlight of it all... the craic with your teammates, meeting all the supporters, and soaking up that winning feeling.

Our campaign that year brought us to Croke Park twice, which I suppose is not something Roscommon teams get to do too often. We were lucky in the first match against Mayo, though strangely we could have won it too. Then, as everyone predicted – well, everyone except us – we were hammered in the replay. It was often said you only got one chance against teams like Mayo, and whoever said that was right as it turned out.

We were at a stage where we really just wanted to win a game in the last eight at Croke Park... and, unfortunately, Roscommon is still at that stage! Everyone is dying to win that championship match at Croker and get to an All-Ireland semi-final. In that first game I remember thinking we had a huge chance, but we just didn't take it. The second day was hugely disappointing. It was like one of those games in Castlebar where the game is over so quickly having been so good the previous day. Of course, people will say Mayo had struggled through the qualifiers and were tired when they met Roscommon in that first match. Maybe that is true. I can't argue with that. They obviously did refocus and came out that second day with more energy, a different plan, and just completely overran us.

It certainly wasn't the case that we were happy enough with our Connacht title. Not at all. From 2016 on, winning a provincial title wasn't enough and I don't think it's enough for the current crop of players either. We *really* wanted to get to an All-Ireland semi-final. It didn't happen for me, but I hope it happens soon for Roscommon because it would be very disappointing for a lot of the players I've played with if the likes of Ciaráin Murtagh, Enda Smith, Diarmuid Murtagh, and those guys don't make it to a semi-final.

While we didn't win an All-Ireland senior title or even reach a semi-final during my time with Roscommon, I don't think there was a whole lot more I could have done as a player. I was very fortunate in terms of the success we had; the amount of playing time I got… the big games I was involved in, and the calibre of players I marked. It was always a challenge, whether I was playing wing-back or wing-forward.

Peter Harte and Johnny Heaney are two players I always think of because any time we played Tyrone or Galway I was tasked with marking either of those. There were definitely games we could have played better in or could have won. There was another Connacht final against Galway at the Hyde and that first quarter-final against Mayo. Those are the game where you think, *Jesus, how did we not win that?*

Looking back over my Roscommon career, there were also aspects of the game I didn't enjoy. I'm glad to see the regimental side of football has been relaxed. Earlier in my career, coming off the back of the early 00s and the success of teams like Armagh and Tyrone, everything was watched. I know people think that happens now, but it's done in a different way. Back then, there was no responsibility given to the players.

For example, you had drinking bans at that time, which thankfully don't really exist anymore. It's now left up to the players. They know if they have training Tuesday night what they need to do. If you want to go out for a drink on Sunday night that's up to you… as long as you can train properly during the week. Before, Jesus even if I was just going into town with my friends and not drinking, someone would see me and assume I was. Next thing they'd ring the manager. That's what it was like for a while.

Even your diet before a match… I remember we were staying away for a match one time. We were supposed to be having scrambled eggs, beans and toast or whatever it was for breakfast, and here I was trying to sneak a sausage and a rasher! There was a big deal made of that and there were questions asked. I remember just thinking, *Is a sausage really the reason we're going to lose?*

Thankfully, I think that side of the game has eased off now and the players have more independence. We're all adults at the end of the day. Set the framework for the players to succeed and then let them do their own thing after that. No one person is the same and everyone should be allowed to thrive as an individual within the team. Players know that if they're not training well, then they won't be picked for games on Saturday and Sunday. They know what they need to do, and I think that's a much better way of doing business.

At the moment, I don't miss playing county football because I'm still involved with my club, Kilbride. I think if I finished playing for club and county at the same time, I would probably miss the game. But I'm still going to training two and three times a week and playing matches. That's all I ever wanted to do… go kick a football around the place, train, play matches… and go home. I didn't always enjoy every aspect of football, as I've said, but I was always there early before training and matches just kicking a ball. Even if there was a loose football lying around between drills, I was the one kicking it in and annoying the goalkeeper. I just wanted to kick a football. When that stops for me that's when I'll miss it.

And I have to say, I really enjoyed watching Roscommon in 2023 as a supporter and no more than our 2017 quarter-final against Mayo, it was awfully disappointing in the end, but I suppose that's for another day!

ENDA SMITH

ROSCOMMON 2-22 ★ ARMAGH 1-19
All-Ireland SFC Qualifier
O'Moore Park, Portlaoise
JULY 7, 2018

★ **ROSCOMMON:** C Lavin; S McDermott, N McInerney, P Domican; J McManus, N Daly, D Murray; T O'Rourke, E Smith (2-1); C Murtagh (0-6,), N Kilroy, C Devaney (0-1); D Smith (0-3), D Murtagh (0-6), C Cregg (0-3). Subs: G Patterson for Domican, Finbar Cregg for C Murtagh, C Compton (0-1) for D Smith, C Daly for McDermott, Fintan Cregg (0-1) for Kilroy.

★ **ARMAGH:** B Hughes; P Burns, B Donaghy, G McCabe; M Shields (1-0), R Owens, S Sheridan (0-1); C Vernon, C Mackin; R McShane (0-1), J Hall (0-1), N Grimley (0-5); R Grugan (0-5), A Murnin (0-4), A Forker (0-1). Subs: J McElroy for McCabe, R McQuillan for Sheridan, N Rowland for Donaghy, G McParland (0-1) for Mackin (52).

WHEN I FIRST broke into the Roscommon senior set-up in 2013, the whole culture around Gaelic football was that *More is Better*. Coaches would dog the life out of lads. But as the years went on, that has thankfully changed, and it's become very much *Less is More*.

I think modern managers have come to the realisation that lads have other things going on in their lives outside of football. Don't get me wrong, you still work *very* hard, but there's definitely more of a balance there now. It's small things like allowing lads to go enjoy social gatherings after league or championship games. There was none of that in 2013. Whereas now, there is a more relaxed approach and I think it's for the better. It's better for the whole panel. That's been the one major change for me.

In terms of the training and the way the game's gone, it's become a lot more

THE ACTION

★★★★★

DESPITE THE SEARING heat at O'Moore Park, this was end-to-end from the start, and it was soon obvious that we were witnessing a genuine contender for 'Game of the Season'. The first-half featured some breathtaking football. Rory Grugan and Andrew Murnin hit 0-4 apiece for Armagh, with all of Murnin's scores coming from play.

From a Roscommon point of view, the ever-reliable Ciaráin Murtagh scored 0-5 while Cathal Cregg caused consternation in the Armagh defence with his intelligent play. It was the Rossies who led at the break, thanks mainly to an Enda Smith goal in the 29th minute.

It was also Roscommon who had the better of it after half-time and they outscored their Ulster opponents four points to one in the first 10 minutes. Armagh did have a glorious opportunity to hit back from the penalty spot, however Rory Grugan's spot-kick was well saved by Colm Lavin in the Roscommon goal.

Armagh did raise a green flag two minutes later, as Mark Shields collected a pass from Ryan McShane before smashing his shot into the bottom corner of Lavin's goal. However, it was Roscommon who finished strongest with a late flurry of 1-4, including another Enda Smith goal, and in doing so, sealed their place in the Super Eights at the expense of the Ulstermen.

★★★★★

about the tactical work. Football's probably not as free-flowing or as easy on the eye as spectators would like to see. As a player, and speaking to other players too, I enjoy the tactical element to it, and trying to figure out another team and how to break them down. It makes sense that training would reflect this and so you spend a lot of time perfecting different phases of play. Stuff like opposition kickouts, your own kickouts, and how you defend and attack as a unit is all very important now.

There is a more player-centred approach to preparation too, and more of a focus on the actual person than just the footballer. Something Kevin McStay brought in around 2017 was a team-building exercise we used to do on our away trips or during camps. It was something I think Connacht Rugby did for a time. Basically, a member of the panel or the backroom would stand up and present a 'biography' piece about themselves in front of the group. You'd talk about your life, from the time you were growing up to your involvement in football, and other life experiences. You were learning to see more than just the player or the coach.

It was a great concept. We had some eye-opening biographies throughout the year and heard from lads who had done amazing things in their lives. It was a great way to figure each other out and build that camaraderie that's so important in any team. Everyone bought into it. While football was so important to us, there was a realisation that there were some great things being done outside of it as well.

We had been relegated from Division One in 2017 but bounced straight back up the following year, beating Cavan 4-16 to 4-12 in the Division Two final in March. It was Kevin McStay's second year in sole charge of the team. We also got to the Connacht final, where we played Galway at Dr Hyde Park. That still feels like a final we just left behind us. We played really well against the wind in the first-half and were up by three points at the break. But we didn't really come out for the second-half, and Galway kicked six points in-a-row just after half-time to turn the game on its head. That meant we went into a fourth-round qualifier against Armagh.

I suppose if you were a neutral, that game against Armagh was unbelievable to watch. The one thing I remember vividly from that day was the heat. It was one of the hottest days I've ever played football in. It's like when you arrive in a foreign country on your holidays, and you step off the plane and the heat just *hits* you. Walking out for the warm-up, you were met by that heat and beaming sunshine. It just added to the whole occasion and the championship feel to the match.

The first-half was high scoring, 1-11 to 0-12. It was a really open game. There was a lot of good quality scoring too. I don't think Armagh hit a single wide in that first-half, while I think we may have had a couple. It was back and forth, and end to end. I started slowly enough but got a goal and then a point close to half-time.

The second-half was a complete contrast to the first. It was mad stuff. I was pushed out a bit further to get on some of the kickouts. I actually had to go off on a blood substitution for 10 minutes as well because I got a bang in the eye. That just added to the chaotic nature of the game for me. It was still in the balance right up to the end, mainly because we had spurned good chances in the second-half. On the other hand, Colm Lavin had also saved a penalty from Rory Grugan which was to prove crucial in the end.

Thankfully, we kicked on in the closing minutes with three or four points in-a-row to go three up. Then, as the game was winding down, we won their kickout and I finished for a goal to put the icing on the cake and make sure we'd put the game beyond them.

I had made my debut in 2013 but probably announced myself on the national stage in the 2017 Connacht final under Kevin McStay. My hard running style was always there but I think Kevin and Liam McHale gave me licence and, most importantly, the confidence to utilise it in the biggest games. I knew I had it in me, but I suppose when I was a bit younger there was some criticism of my style of play. There was a suggestion that maybe I held on to the ball a bit too long and that it was bad for the team. In fairness to the two lads, they encouraged me to persevere with it, but also to mix it up a bit too. They always told me it was a strength of mine… 'Don't stop doing what you're good at,' they'd say.

I suppose they looked at it as risk-reward… and the rewards could be great if it went to plan. The years from 2017 to '19 were exciting, and everything seemed new to the panel, including Division One football and regular Connacht titles. Seánie McDermott and Cathal Cregg had been around for a while and probably experienced something like that level of success in 2010, but probably didn't see such a sustained period where we were challenging.

Our success was coming at a time when the game was slightly changing too. Dublin were just so dominant at the time and there seemed to be a huge gap between them and probably Mayo in second place, and then the rest. They were just so far ahead of the other teams for those two or three years. Looking back, we were probably a good bit off those real *top* teams compared to where we are now. We're more mature and probably more aware of what it takes compared to back then, when it was so new to us that we probably didn't realise the size of the gulf in class.

By 2018, I'd been around a few years, so it's only natural that you take on a more leading role in the team. You grow fast into it too because the years go by so quickly. You can be hanging around the county panel doing very little for three or four years and those years are gone, and you're left wondering, *What the hell happened here? What have we achieved?* When you've a good core bunch on the panel you really need to be making hay.

Between 2017 and '19, we just knew we were capable of doing something. The likes of myself and some of the younger players recognised that we were now leaders in the team and needed to be ones to drive it on. Not to be leaving it to lads who had maybe been there before.

My brother, Donie was another one of those 'younger' players who were now leaders. He had gone into the Roscommon senior panel the year before me… and now playing senior club and county football with him is special. It's very hard to picture him not being there, to be honest. We have a good understanding; football is our main topic of conversation about eighty percent of the time anyway! He's good to bounce things off too.

We'd be straight up with each other on whether we're doing the right thing or the wrong thing… on and off the pitch. There's obviously a good level of understanding between us, which comes from years of playing outside in the garden or around the house! We each know what the other one's thinking, and you get that little bounce too knowing you're on the same pitch. Hopefully it can continue for another few years yet.

In 2018, I felt that in a one-off game against *most* teams that we could give anyone a right good game of it. But at that time, we sometimes found it difficult to put in back-to-back performances against the top teams. That was probably down to squad depth and experience. Some teams were just much further on than us in terms of conditioning and other aspects. If you look at the previous year, we lost out to Mayo in a replay, hammered on the day. But the first day out we felt it was there for us, and that could have been a door to an All-Ireland semi-final. Mayo were pretty much at the peak of their powers by then, and just lost to Dublin by a kick of a ball that year. I think it was a good experience, but we just found it hard to put those *big* performances in consistently.

I'm not looking to play the 'young team' card, but we probably did lack that bit of experience and strength in depth. In the Super Eights in 2018, we were well beaten by Tyrone in the first game. Then we played Donegal in the Hyde, and it was a comfortable win for them. The Super Eights never really took off for us, whereas if it was a one-off game to get to a semi-final it might have been tighter. Who knows? It was tough at the time because we were getting well beaten, but it definitely did stand to us in the long run. It brought us that realisation of where we were and what was ahead of us if we ever wanted to close the gap.

I think that consistency against the top teams has always been a major issue for us. But I think in 2023 we definitely showed we are capable of it. Even on days when we didn't play brilliantly, we were still well in contention. We didn't ship any big scores or take any tankings. It was usually a point either way against the bigger teams. In the league, we didn't play well against Mayo at the Hyde, but were still in it and could have sneaked a result right up to the end. That's huge for us as a team.

Obviously, we were gutted losing the games against Kildare and Cork in the championship. It was made even more disappointing due to the fact that we went into both those games as heavy favourites. We would have liked to think we had reached the stage that while those games were going to be tough, we'd have enough about us to deal with both of those teams. There was a point in the difference in those two games, so you're talking about the finest of margins between going out of the championship and reaching an All-Ireland quarter-final. When it's as tight as that, it's often hard to pinpoint one decision or one mistake in a game. It could be a whole load of things. It wasn't like we suffered a heavy beating against anyone or looked out of our depth, so I didn't do a whole load of soul-searching in the months after the championship, thinking *What the hell I am at?* I just put it down to experience and vowed to put it right in 2024.

Looking at the bigger picture, I love playing for Roscommon and that's the main reason I do it. I've been a part of the Roscommon senior team since 2013, and I'm there year-in, year-out. I'm still enjoying it. I like the challenge and the routine of it.

I also love putting myself up against the best players, and best teams... just putting yourself out there and getting every last ounce out of yourself in terms of training and performances in games. Of course, it's all about the great days and the memories, and thankfully we've had plenty of those in the last 10 years or so.

Even the league games at the Hyde in 2023 were rocking. To bring it full circle from that day in 2018, there was an unbelievable buzz after the Armagh game this year, in particular. I don't think there's many other ways you can replicate that feeling. I get it from sport and from football, and I know Donie and the rest of my teammates do too. That's the main reason we play and why we keep coming back year after year... after year.

And, as long as we're able, and the bodies remain in relatively good shape, then we'll keep coming back... sure what else would you expect us to do?

Printed in Great Britain
by Amazon

34340390R00118